M000040427

0000 8192971

09901255296

0000416935

As church leadership continues to access the proliferation of scholarly works on so many varying aspects of the Church and the believer's faith walk, there is a growing need for a return to responsible and scholarly revelations on the core principles of spiritual warfare. *Demons Are Subject to Us* by Pastor Isidore Agoha is a must-read for every believer that understands and wisely submits to God's call and the principles He has established for us in the expansion plan of the kingdom of God. It is clear that this author is a man of God displaying true integrity, who reveals the efficacy of these principles amidst the backdrop of spiritual and social turbulence of this twenty-first century society.

—BISHOP CARLTON T. BROWN
SENIOR PASTOR, BETHEL GOSPEL ASSEMBLY, NEW YORK
AUTHOR, *TILL DEATH DO WE S.H.O.P*

Demons Are Subject to Us is true to the scriptural texts on the subject matter. It serves to elucidate the topic, giving the average Christian in the current high-tech humanistic environment a good handle on the issue so that he/she does not need to be ignorantly and powerlessly at the mercy of demons. With his background in medicine, the author has been able to give valuable insight into how some of the disease entities we battle can be linked to these nefarious influences.

—REV. DR. RUTH C. ONUKWUE
MISSIONARY/EXECUTIVE DIRECTOR
BETHEL GOSPEL ASSEMBLY MINISTRIES
SOUTH AFRICA

DEM●NS

ARE
SUBJECT
TO
US

Isidore
AGOHA

CREATION
HOUSE
A STRANG COMPANY

Demons Are Subject to Us by Isidore Agoha
Published by Creation House
A Strang Company
600 Rinehart Road
Lake Mary, Florida 32746
www.strangbookgroup.com

Unless otherwise noted, Scripture quotations are from the New American Standard Bible-Updated Edition, Copyright © 1960, 1962, 1963, 1968, 1971, 1972, 1973, 1975, 1977, 1995 by The Lockman Foundation. Used by permission. (www.Lockman.org)

Scripture quotations marked KJV are from the King James Version of the Bible.

Design Director: Bill Johnson

Cover design by Justin Evans

Library of Congress Control Number: 2009931068
International Standard Book Number: 978-1-59979-889-9

09 10 11 12 13 — 9 8 7 6 5 4 3 2
Printed in the United States of America

CONTENTS

ACKNOWLEDGMENTS

THE SUCCESSFUL PUBLICATION of this seminal book on such a sensitive subject is not merely a literary success. For me it is a spiritual breakthrough. Through the course of working on this project I was blessed with the kind support of God's people, and I must humbly admit my inability to recall the names of all who through their words of encouragement, prayers, and other forms of support to my wife, my children, and me allowed God to use them to bring this vision to reality.

Working on a book manuscript is always an arduous task, but thank God I had the very helpful hands and skills of Sister Viola Julien, Brother Anthony Omokha, Sister Doreen Nelson, and Sister Rita Abies Omokha.

I will remain grateful for the initial editorial reviews of Sister Dawn Jackson and Rev. Wendy Trott.

The pastoral covering and support of Elder Carlton T. Brown and Bishop Ezra Williams, both of Bethel Gospel Assembly, New York, have been invaluable.

I am greatly appreciative of my assistant, Pastor Michael Desmond Hickinson, Minister Sue Smith Vaughn, and the entire ministerial staff at Triumphant Life Church (TLC), Bronx, for their labor of love and commitment to ministry that allowed me time for this work.

I thank the Lord for the intercessory cover of Minister Olga James and the team of intercessors at TLC, and for His prophetic confirmation through His minister Pauline Okoroji.

I am forever indebted to my wife and associate in ministry, Maureen, and my children Ebuka, Chika, and Ifeanyi for their understanding and support.

Finally, all glory and adoration go to Jehovah, the Lord God Almighty, who, through His Son the Lord Jesus Christ and by the anointing of His Spirit, called me to this ministry. May His plans and purposes for this calling be fulfilled. Amen!

—Isidore A. Agoha
New York City
July 2009

PROLOGUE

UNTIL THE 1980s and early 1990s, there was a great dearth of books and teachings on the subject of deliverance and demonology. Also, there was a relative degree of ignorance, apathy, confusion, unbelief, and cynicism surrounding this subject. When many sections of the church are confronted with a deliverance ministry, they still respond in the same way those in the Capernaum synagogue reacted to the deliverance ministry of the Lord Jesus, namely:

> What is this? A new teaching with authority! He commands even the unclean spirits, and they obey Him.
>
> —MARK 1:27

This is the degree of ignorance that existed among God's people more than two thousand years ago concerning the ministry of deliverance in the Lord's name. Unfortunately, such ignorance has survived among many in the church today. Therefore, I have written this book, not to add to the long list of books on deliverance and demonology in circulation, but to help overcome ignorance, apathy, confusion, unbelief, and cynicism. Having overcome these obstacles, the reader will gain a new insight concerning certain negative experiences in his or her personal life, and will not only receive deliverance, but proceed to walk in dominion over demons.

I have chosen the title *Demons Are Subject to Us* because my emphasis is not on mere deliverance from demons, but the divine ability and freedom to cast out demons through the dominion of Christ in our lives in order to serve God effectively. This is not only a book for those needing deliverance from demons; it is also an introduction for ministers of the gospel of the kingdom and church workers who are being led to work in the ministry of deliverance.

This book is a product of systematic Bible study and a personal experience in the ministry of deliverance and healing spanning almost two decades. This book is by no means God's last word on the subject of deliverance from demons, but I believe it is a helpful tool in the hands of ministers and deliverance workers. I sought to keep it as scriptural and objective as possible by the guidance of the Lord. Yet certain things may appear or sound subjective, since personal experiences are by nature subjective. With this in mind, I suggest that you prayerfully ask for the Lord's guidance.

Finally, I commit this book and every user to the revelation and power of the Holy Spirit so that the Lord might fulfill His purposes through His Word in this book.

THE MIRACLE OF DELIVERANCE

T HE MOST GLORIOUS reality in the theme of demonology is that we who believe in Christ Jesus can now effectively exercise authority, victory, and dominion over demons. Moreover, it is my personal belief that this is one of the most amazing privileges offered to the New-Testament believer through the triumphant ministry of the Lord Jesus Christ. The believer's authority to cast out demons, when appropriately exercised, demonstrates a core aspect of the reversal of the Fall. This reality essentially buttresses the fact that we do not have to remain under demonic bondage any longer; rather, we are now equipped by the Lord through the power of the Holy Spirit to keep demons under subjection. This was the great discovery made by the seventy disciples whom the Lord Jesus sent out to preach the gospel of the kingdom. In their missionary report they noted, "Lord, even the demons are subject to us in your name" (Luke 10:17).

Apparently, there is a tone of surprise in the disciples' comment revealed by their opening word, *even*. And for the first time, humanity tasted the dawn of a new era of authority and dominion known as the Kingdom of God. This new order puts Satan and his demons under the dominion of the believer in Christ. After the Fall and for the rest of the old creation, Satan and his demons had usurped the God-given authority and dominion of the first Adam. They had historically exercised this dominion to perpetuate corruption and other manifestations of the Fall such as sin, death, sickness, shame, humiliation, poverty, and vanity. And this new order of dominion and authority that the disciples had just tasted was going to be a vital and lasting feature of the new creation and the kingdom that Jesus—the Last Adam, and the Christ—was about to inaugurate. The Lord Himself gave them cause for more surprise and excitement when He said in response:

> I was watching Satan fall from heaven like lightning. Behold, I have given you authority to tread upon serpents and scorpions, and over all the power of the enemy and nothing shall injure you. Nevertheless do not rejoice in this, that the spirits are subject to you, but rejoice that your names are recorded in heaven.
> —Luke 10:18–19

By His response, the Lord reveals three great truths about the condition of the New Creation in Christ. First, Satan had fallen and lost the authority Adam had ceded to him through the Fall. Second, humankind would now in Christ receive redemption from sin and the dominion of Satan. Third, humans, having been freed from satanic captivity, will now proceed to exercise dominion over the earth. Consequently Satan and the entire kingdom of darkness are now subject to the church.

This reality, which brought great amazement to the disciples, was not without impact on the Lord's own emotion and spirit. He rejoiced and praised the Father for such grace and such a miracle. At that very time He rejoiced greatly in the Holy Spirit and said, "I praise thee, O Father, Lord of heaven and earth, that thou did hide these things from the wise and intelligent and reveal them to babes. Yes, Father, for thus it is well pleasing in your sight" (Luke 10:21).

This expression of great joy and praise by the Lord Jesus in this situation underscores the importance and value God places on the redeemed person's dominion over satanic forces and also over the earth. This is probably the most exciting and celebrated moment in the Lord's earthly life and ministry in the record of the New Testament. I believe He still rejoices in this way any time the church exercises dominion over demons and casts them out. This clearly reveals the value of the deliverance ministry before God.

GOD'S PURPOSE AT CREATION

The deliverance ministry is indeed a great victory for both God and the church, especially when it is viewed in light of God's purposes at creation and the events leading up to Adam's Fall, as well as the change of fortunes after it. At creation, God had ordained that humans should have dominion over the whole earth and all created things. Satan had rebelled against God, and the earth had come under corruption and judgment. Humans were God's appointed monarchs over the earth; they received a kingdom and a mandate from God to conquer and subdue the earth for the Lord God, and also to guard it from Satan's control and influences. However, through deception we lost the life of God in us and also our God-given kingdom and dominion. God would therefore visit the earth, Satan and humankind with judgment (Genesis 1:24–28).

CREEPING THINGS—SERPENTS AND SCORPIONS

Of the creatures over which humans were to exercise dominion, "creeping things" received an emphatic mention in many passages that deal with demons, deliverance, and dominion. Then God said, "Let us make man in our image, according to our likeness; and let them rule over the fish of the sea and over the bird of the sky, over the cattle and over all the earth, and over every creeping thing that creeps on the earth" (Gen. 1:26).

Obviously, Lucifer who came in as the serpent was persona non grata in the earth of Adam's dominion. It is no accident therefore, that the Lord said to the serpent, "Because you have done this, cursed are you more than all cattle, and more than every beast of the field; on your belly shall you go and dust shall you eat" (Gen. 2:14).

Clearly, not only was the serpent irredeemably cursed more than any other beast, it was thereafter doomed to creep on its belly and feed on dust for the rest of its life. This curse immediately set off a long-lasting enmity between humans, who are made of dust (Gen. 3:19), and the serpent that was now bound to feed on dust.

The serpent's insatiable appetite for dust has made us his food. Hence in all of our history, we have always been infested, corrupted and "fed upon" by the serpent that creeps upon the surface of the earth. Through this depraved condition, Satan has exercised dominion over the earth and over humankind since the Fall. The fallen humanity made of dust could neither resist nor fight back. Redemption was now only possible through the seed of the woman—the last Adam, the Messiah that was to come, since the first Adam hopelessly failed at redeeming himself or God's creation (Gen. 3:15; 1 Cor. 15:45–47). Only the Lord Jesus Christ, God's perfect Man from heaven, could exercise dominion over the serpent because in His eternal nature He had no dust in Him. This is why He could boldly declare, "The ruler of this world (Satan) is coming, and he has nothing in me" (John 14:30).

Yet the Lord is not content to be the only Son of glory to the Father. His goal is to be "first among many brethren" (Rom.

8:29), and to "bring many sons to glory" (Heb. 2:10). So when the Lord Jesus—God's typical Man—came, He did a "test drive" with the seventy disciples, whom He sent out with an impartation of His heavenly royalty. He gave his evaluation of their successful exercise of dominion over demons: "I saw Satan fall...and I give you power over serpents and scorpions and nothing shall hurt you" (Luke 10:18–19).

What the seventy discovered in essence is a miracle—impartation of divine grace whereby we are now not only free from the dominion of demons but also actually have authority over them and over the earth in the Lord's name. The church henceforth ceases to be food to creeping things. The initiative concerning the governance of the earth is now with us, the church, and no longer with Satan and his creeping agents. The tables are now turned.

This is indeed revelation of a great breakthrough in the spirit realm when we realize that God's people of previous dispensations, including the prophets and kings, wished they could experience such a wonder of redemption and of the new creation. They had only seen it in visions and prophesied it, but now for the church it is reality and history in the making. The kingdom Adam lost is now at hand, restored in Christ to the church (Matt. 11:11–12; Luke 1:1–24).

They Shall Take Up Serpents

In the words of the Great Commission, it is said that those who believe in the Lord will take up serpents. With this authority and dominion, the church will conquer, subdue, and guard the earth from demons. The miracle of casting out of demons is indeed a unique miracle for the church. It is a divine grace imparted only to the church of the Lord Jesus Christ. No other nation of people in the history of creation has received such a grace. Neither angels nor the Old Covenant people received such grace from God. Indeed, the blessings of New Testament salvation are immeasurably wondrous. The great apostle Peter describes this salvation in the following words:

> In this you greatly rejoice…obtaining as the outcome of your faith the salvation of your souls. As to this salvation, the prophets who prophesied of the grace that would come to you made careful search and inquiry, seeking to know what person or time the Spirit of Christ within them was indicating as He predicted the sufferings of Christ and the glories to follow. It was revealed to them that they were not serving themselves, but you in these things which now have been announced to you through those who preached the gospel to you by the Holy Spirit sent from heaven, things into which angels long to look.
>
> —1 Peter 1:9–12

I believe that the ministry of deliverance is one of those unique things given to the church as an outcome of our salvation through faith; so unique that the prophets of old and the angels did prophesy and announce them, and now they look on to see the church move in the power of the Holy Spirit exercising grace to a dying world. The greatness of New Testament salvation is also described in the epistle to the Hebrews, "How shall we escape if we neglect so great a salvation? After it was at the first spoken through the Lord, it was confirmed to us by those who heard, God also bearing witness with them, both by signs and wonders and by various miracles and by gifts of the Holy Spirit according to His own will" (Heb. 2:4).

It is no accident that these verses opened with a warning

about negligence of our uniquely great salvation. The greatness is based on the fact that it was originally handed down to us by the Lord Himself, confirmed by the apostles, and attested to by signs, wonders, miracles and gifts of the Holy Spirit. It is most encouraging to note that the Lord has not withdrawn His Word and that the testimony of the apostles abides with us. It only remains for the church to take up the salvation and the kingdom given to it by the Lord and keep demons under subjection on the earth. This is the Lord's desire, and for that I pray this:

> *O Lord Father, God of heaven and earth, may your church now on the earth see this grace of deliverance from demons and dominion over Satan's kingdom the way You and Your Son our Lord see it, and use it to regain Your kingdom on the earth. Amen!*

2

AN ENCOUNTER WITH DEMONS

T HERE IS ONE incident believed by many to be the first public encounter between Jesus Christ and demons. This incident, which was recorded in Mark 1:21–28 and Luke 4:31–37, also provokes an examination of some basic principles of demonology and spiritual warfare. Furthermore, there are some valuable spiritual lessons that are very relevant and up-to-date with the experience of the present-day Christian and religious people as a whole. Let us, therefore, explore the key aspects of this encounter and identify the appropriate principles of demonology.

A MAN WITH AN UNCLEAN SPIRIT

And they went into Capernaum and immediately on the Sabbath He entered the synagogue and began to teach. And they were amazed at His teaching for He was teaching them as one having authority and not as the scribes. Just then there was a man in their synagogue with an unclean spirit and he cried out saying, "What do we have to do with you, Jesus of Nazareth? Have you come to destroy us? I know who you are—the Holy one of God!" And Jesus rebuked him, saying, "Be quiet and come out of him." And throwing him into convulsions, the unclean spirit cried out with a loud voice, and came out of him. And they were all amazed so that they debated among themselves saying, "What this is? A new teaching with authority! He commands even the unclean spirits and they obey Him." And immediately the news about Him went out everywhere into all the surrounding districts of Galilee.

—MARK 1:21–28

The first lesson here is that the ultimate victim of demons in this case, and in most other cases discussed in the New Testament, is a human being. It is a very clear fact of Scripture that humans came under demonic domination as a result of Adam's Fall. Man's subjection under demonic bondage is one of the major consequences of the Fall of Adam and Eve. Prior to the Fall, all things, including demons, were subject to humans (Gen. 1:26–27; 9:2).

The second lesson is that people who are afflicted by demons are not necessarily obvious "sinners" or outcasts of a religious community. The man with the unclean spirit in the center of this first synagogue encounter was by all accounts not without religion. He was, apparently, a practicing Jew, as he was attending synagogue on a Sabbath day. He must have attended many of these synagogue services, yet he was troubled by demons. In the midst of all his religious involvements and observances, these demons found place and comfort in their victim. He was still bound and under some form of torment. This man is a classic picture of many religious people, who still do not have Jesus or who have not appropriated God's grace, including deliverance in Jesus.

Now, the entrance of Jesus into that synagogue is typical of the deliverance ministry that manifests when He comes into a religious life, or into a family, marriage, ministry, career, business, or local church. Demons do not mind religiosity or piety as long as Jesus is not invited and acknowledged. Furthermore, religious complacency, lukewarm attitudes, false religious hopes, and wrong religious motives—including religious politics and other wrong internal and external religious attitudes—will only negatively impact the lives of those involved so as to render them conducive to demonic hibernation. True freedom and hope in religion only come through personal repentance toward God and faith in the Lord Jesus Christ. Any religious activities that negate these two most basic divine requirements are indeed "dead works" (Heb. 6:1), which like dead bodies stink and can only attract demons, the way the carcasses draw vultures (Matt. 24:28).

A CONFLICT OF SPIRITS

This encounter was also primarily a spiritual confrontation. On the physical, sensory level it would seem that Jesus was directly dealing with the man. However, in spiritual reality, Jesus by the anointing of the Holy Spirit was dealing with the demons in the man. It was a confrontation between the sovereign Holy Spirit and the evil spirits (demons) in that man.

This is the basis of spiritual warfare. In its very nature, spiritual warfare is not of flesh and blood (human entities), but against "spiritual forces of wickedness" among other evil supernatural entities (Eph. 6:12). However, we must also recognize that human entities do get involved as channels of expression of the desires or activities of these unseen spiritual forces.

The most important lesson about spiritual confrontation brought out in this passage is that evil forces do not aspire to engage in any form of combat with the Lord Jesus Christ. On the basis of biblical revelation and personal ministry experience, it seems to me that any time they do come into direct spiritual contact with the Lord they always express some form of shock and panic. Their confessions during this encounter typically reveal their helplessness in the Lord's presence, "What do we have to do with you, Jesus of Nazareth?" (Mark 1:24).

In other words, they do not expect to come so close to Jesus Christ, the holiness of God personified. They know that the holiness of Jesus is absolutely contrary to their unholy and evil nature. In this example, the demons reasoned further that since the holiness of God revealed in Jesus would not tolerate the iniquity and wickedness in them, they had only one prospect: their sudden, non-negotiable expulsion from the man and some form of subsequent judgment.

This reasoning by those demons gave rise to their follow-up question: "Have you come to destroy us?" (Mark 1:24). It is a fact that the presence of Jesus always spells one expectation for them—expulsion! And one destiny—destruction! Often the expulsion is in the present time and the destruction is in future.

Very clearly, demons understand the holiness of and anointing in Jesus. Satan and his forces never assail this holiness and anointing. All evil forces, including Satan, bow and surrender when the holiness and anointing of Jesus are made manifest. The holiness, anointing, glory and all of God's fullness in the Son are encapsulated in the name *Jesus*. This is the name above all names to which every knee must bow and which every tongue must confess (Phil. 2:8–10). Through God's grace, those who walk in His holiness and anointing are also able in this day and age to challenge Satan and his forces in any form of spiritual combat, effectively pulling down Satan's stronghold.

In summarizing this lesson, the key principle is that Satan and his forces can only exercise power, authority and control when and where the authority and rule of Jesus is not proclaimed and established. When and where the reign of Jesus is made manifest, demons not only cease to exert their influence but also seek exit. In order to keep their place and influence, therefore, demons will use all sorts of devices, including fear, ignorance, unbelief, sin, prayerlessness, unforgiveness, materialism, and false religion, to obscure the truth of the power and authority of Jesus Christ.

When a Christian fully comes under the holiness and anointing of the Lord Jesus Christ, walking in the discipline of character, prayer, praise, testimony of the power of His blood, faith in the cross, and the power of the Holy Spirit with proclamation through evangelism, demons will be subjected to the same harassment and defeat that they received in the hand of Jesus. This is the will and purpose of the Lord in the Great Commission (Mark 16:14–18).

SUPERNATURAL KNOWLEDGE

Demons are supernatural in nature because they are spirits. However, they certainly have nothing divine about their nature. The Holy Spirit is supernatural; but more than that, He is divine, sovereign, and pure. The supernatural nature and power of demons is of a corrupt and impure source: Satan.

During the encounter with the man with the unclean spirit, one supernatural attribute clearly demonstrated by demons was knowledge. They expressed some form of knowledge about Jesus that can only be appreciated by supernatural perception, identifying Jesus as a Nazarene and as the "Holy One of God." They also recognized His power to judge them. These are spiritual truths that can only be received or perceived by supernatural revelation. Yet at a time when Jesus had not yet announced those details about Himself, and while the religious audience had not yet appreciated those truths, these demons had already grasped them. Moreover, this has much to do with the origin and age of demons. I believe that demons were part of the pre-Adamic age and may have access to some truths from that era. However, this form of supernatural knowledge needs to be further examined.

First, this expression of supernatural knowledge does not make demons honest and reliable. They are not the authors of such spiritual truths; they only confess them in moments of stress. This pattern is repeated in the ministry of Jesus in the Gadarenes (Mark 5:1–10; Luke 8:26–34) and in the ministry of Paul in Philippi (Acts 16:16–21). Both Jesus and Paul exercised great discernment in each case and proceeded to do God's will by casting the demons out. Neither the Lord nor Paul was excited, impressed, or distracted by such deep revelations about their persons and ministry. Their example emphasizes the need for Christians to exercise discernment on a regular basis. God in His wisdom empowered the church with His gift of discerning of spirits. We need to understand that the church in this age is being confronted with a degree of deception capable of swaying the elect if God doesn't intervene. Revelation of truth is never to be used to lead people away from the true God; it is to be used in bringing people to God.

Second, the demons' expression of supernatural knowledge could not change them or save them from being expelled or from final judgment. Their knowledge could not lead them to willing submission and, therefore, was devoid of worship. All claims to the true knowledge of God must culminate in the submission to and worship of God the Father through Jesus Christ the Son. Any purported knowledge or revelation from God that does not lead to submission to and worship of Jesus as Lord does not attract God's blessing, but invariably leads to judgment. Satan, fallen angels, and demons are incapable of such willing worship.

Third, these beings' incapability of voluntary worship and submission is underscored by their failure to address Jesus as Lord. They addressed Jesus by many titles, but never as Lord! (See also Luke 8:26–39 and Mark 8:28–34.) This, I believe, is because lordship demands worship through personal, voluntary submission. However, Satan and his forces never willingly submit to Jesus Christ as Lord. They are incapable of it because they are incapable of repentance and change, and are already doomed for judgment since they have no hope of salvation. The real feeling their supernatural knowledge produced in them is revealed by James the apostle as follows, "Demons know there is one God but they tremble" (James 2:19).

As I understand it, the knowledge of the reality of God for Satan and his forces is tormenting. They "tremble" or shudder at such a blessed reality; and any feeling or emotion expressed as a shudder is certainly not a blessing but a repulsive emotional response to a terrible past, present, or future experience. In this case, demons shudder because the reality of the person of God reminds them of the judgment awaiting them at the second coming of Jesus.

On the other hand, the same reality of God's existence is capable of bringing about a transformation to even the worst human offender, since humans are still capable of repentance toward God and faith in Jesus Christ (Acts 20:21; Heb. 6:1–3). This potential attitude in us can release God's grace of forgiveness and the fullness of all of His inheritance. In this way, God still accepts us. The ultimate lesson is that although the door of salvation has been shut against Satan and his spirit cohorts, God's salvation is still open to fallen humanity. This salvation is by repentance and faith in Jesus Christ as Savior and Lord. In the final analysis, Jesus is Lord over all, including Satan and his spirit allies, because God has made all His enemies His footstool (Psalm 2; 110:1–3).

PLURALITY OF PERSONS

Another clearly emergent and important aspect of this encounter is the plurality of persons in at least two respects.

First, the man himself is a different entity from the demons in him. In Mark 1:23, he is described as a "man with an unclean spirit." In other words, there is a clear separation between the man (a person) and the unclean spirit (another person). Both entities are persons; neither of them is less than a personality.

This fact is underscored by the way Jesus dealt with them. He said, "Be quiet and come out of him," addressing the demon in the man. When the demon was thus dealt with, the man regained his freedom. This is another level of discernment demonstrated by Jesus, which is alien to much of the present materialistic mindset in today's church. As far as Jesus is concerned, demons are real persons with real identity and intelligible activity. Demons and other spiritual entities are not imaginary or nebulous figures.

In dealing with people in need, Christian ministers will be challenged to seek the discerning power of the Holy Spirit in order to be able to precisely identify the real spiritual enemy at work. Also, in our relationships, this discernment will be of tremendous value in assisting us to separate human persons and the forces at work in them—both of the Holy Spirit or evil spirits.

The second aspect of this plurality of persons is the fact that within the identity of the demon, there is a change from the singular to the plural. At one stage of the conversation the demon interchangeably uses the pronouns *we* and *us* to describe itself and its nature, suggesting the influence of more than one. At another stage within the same verse, it switches to the pronoun *I* (Mark 1:24). The following conclusions may be drawn from this observation:

- The use of personal pronouns underscores the personality of demons.

- Demons operate in groups or gangs ranging to thousands or more. In the case of the Gadarene demoniac, discussed in Mark 5:1–14, the stated number was "legion," meaning at least six thousand demons. It is indeed scary but true that one individual can accommodate such a number of demons in his or her personality.

- The human personality and body has a capacity to accommodate spirits. Apart from the human spirit, which is an indigenous part of every human body, the human body is a receptacle of spirits. When yielded to the Lord Jesus Christ, it is a well of streams of living waters capable of turning out rivers of the Holy Spirit (John 7:37). In his letter to the church at Corinth, Paul describes the body as a temple of the Holy Spirit. Likewise, when yielded to Satan, legions of demons can have legal tenancy in a human body. In any case, spirits— holy or evil—crave the human personality and body. The choice is yours to receive the Holy Spirit by yielding to Jesus, or to receive evil spirits by yielding to Satan (Rom. 6:16).

Finally, as a lesson, the prevailing religious attitude, which fails to recognize demons as spirit persons or entities, and the secular mindset of denying the supernatural were far from the attitude of Jesus and the early church. If demons were not real persons, Jesus would not have given them specific orders and expected them to respond. To that synagogue audience, the reality of demons had long been established before that incident. What was new and amazing was the method of Jesus" in dealing with demons.

PHYSICAL REACTIONS

The manifestation of physical reactions in the demonized man following the command issued by the Lord Jesus presents yet another important lesson in demonology. In the case under review, the physical reactions include:

- a (loud) cry

- speech: "What do we have to do with you?"

- falling under power

- convulsions

- expulsion.

There are other forms of physical reactions observable during deliverance sessions. These are essentially activities of the invisible indwelling demons. However, they are usually manifested to the human senses through the various physical body parts of their victim. In this case, I would suppose the body parts mostly used by these demons include the voice and the entire body. We can therefore sum it up as the material expression of the unseen demons in the man.

A New Teaching with Authority

The demon(s) and the man possessed were not the only individuals affected by Jesus' authority. The synagogue audience was also greatly impacted by this whole incident. Their response could be summed up in one word: amazement! This amazement elicited a common question among the audience: "What is this?" I believe that "this" was a reference to the dramatic, supernatural, life-changing result produced by the ministry of Jesus within minutes. The people offered an inspired explanation when they described it as a "new doctrine" (Mark 1:27). More literally, the New American Standard Bible translates, "a new doctrine with authority."

Interestingly, shortly before this encounter, people had observed that Jesus was teaching as one with authority. His teaching was certainly on a different level from that of their scribes. Likewise, His approach to demonology and the quality of the results was completely strange. By their own testimony of a "new teaching with authority" these synagogue goers seem to imply that nobody, beginning with the ministry of the patriarchs through the prophets, judges, kings, priests and other Old Testament saints, ever dealt with demons the way the Lord Jesus did.

In fact, in the Old Testament dispensations, there was no servant of God known to have had a deliverance ministry in the way and measure with which Jesus and His servants were endowed. The Old Testament believers did know that demons existed, but they did not have a deliberate and strategic or systematic ministry of casting demons out on a consistent basis. King David could qualify as someone who came close to this ministry in the Old Testament, however his was not a direct ministry of deliverance. Furthermore, I believe David's was only a picture of the perfect ministry of deliverance to be established in his promised seed, Jesus the Messiah. The lesson here also is that the ministry of deliverance is a unique gift of the Father to the church through Jesus Christ.

Although exorcism was in vogue during the time of Jesus, the audience saw the style and method of Jesus as unique and incomparable, especially in the sense of efficacy. They discerned the divine attestation to the ministry of Jesus. By implication also, they discovered the impotence of the claims of their contemporary exorcists and the scribes. On these grounds, therefore, one could appreciate the awe and other results the ministry of Jesus produced in the man with an unclean spirit and also on the entire synagogue audience.

In the light of these facts, it is unfortunate and regrettable that in the twenty-first century a large section of the church does still ask the question, "What new teaching is this?" even when they are brought face-to-face with this ministry. The degree of spiritual and material deprivation among God's people as a result of the dearth of this ministry is equally incalculable and lamentable. There are indeed millions of traditional and some liturgical exorcists in many parts of the world and in some sections of professing Christendom today; however, they lack the biblical insight and authority with which Jesus endows His true disciples.

Non-biblical exorcism was found to be sterile by the synagogue audience more than two thousand years ago. Today it is still impotent, while also spiritually and often financially fraudulent. The experience of the seven sons of Sceva is one such presumptuous case of non-Christian attempt at the ministry of deliverance (Acts 19:11–17). Much of exorcism as practiced in virtually every part of the world today, especially among animists, witchdoctors, herbalists, native priests, Muslims, and other non-Christian religions, is at variance with New Testament revelation. Also, there are many non-biblical practices involved in exorcism as practiced among some liturgical circles in professing Christendom. Such non-biblical exorcism may involve incantations, enchantments, washings, and other bizarre methods that Jesus and the early church did not employ.

The method of the Lord and His church is simple. It usually involves the proclamation of God's Word in faith and the sovereign power of the Holy Spirit manifested in the person and name of the Lord Jesus.

HIS FAME SPREAD ABROAD

More than the amazement expressed by the synagogue audience, the whole incident of the deliverance of the man with an unclean spirit generated great news—so great that it propelled the ministry of Jesus from obscurity to fame in the whole region of Galilee within hours. The remainder of the Lord's itinerary for the day, which included the healing of Peter's mother-in-law and climaxed in the evening with an evangelistic service, was characterized by many miraculous healings and deliverance. The impact of the news was so effective that it drew the whole city to Peter's door and paved the way for miracles (Mark 1:28-35).

In spreading the news of the Lord's work, the people magnified His name. Through the people's testimony, many who were in need were drawn to Him. The lesson in this case is that when people are drawn to Jesus, their needs are met, their burdens are lifted and they come into His rest. In this rest they receive their inheritance—God's provision for their needs, "Come unto me all who are weary and heavy laden and I will give you rest" (Matt. 11:28).

It is the Lord who gives the invitation, and it is Him also who provides the salvation, healing, and deliverance. But, it is we, His servants, who have the honor of publishing the invitation and the works of the Lord. The people in the days of the Lord's earthly ministry were effective in publishing His work notwithstanding the technological handicap of their era. This, therefore, poses a great challenge to those of us who live in our present high-tech age, abundantly blessed with a polyglot of communication facilities. In the case of the events in this Capernaum synagogue, the whole district or county was reached in one day. However, with the blessing of contemporaneous satellite network television broadcast, that encounter could have been beamed live to every continent. Recorded videotapes and DVD recordings of the same incident could have been used to reach more people, and it could have been translated from the Aramaic language into hundreds of languages of this day.

A study of the context does not necessarily indicate that the disciples of Jesus did the spreading of the news because as of then He had not even raised up to twelve followers. He only had four, namely Simon (Peter), Andrew, James, and John (Mark 1:14–21). It appears that it was those in the synagogue audience who, when they witnessed the miracle, were struck with awe that led them to proclaim the good news.

The life and power of Jesus impacted those unbelievers to such an extent that they not only believed but also immediately began to tell the news of God's power through the Lord Jesus. Likewise, we as the Lord's servants today can impact our world with God's power through our cultivation of the fruit and the gifts of the Holy Spirit so that those who do not believe will not only believe, but will testify that God is real. When the world sees the reality of God and His power in the church, the world will reject humanism, Satanism, new age philosophy, occultism, false religion, and the theory of evolution. They will come to the church's door with their needs for an answer from Jesus.

One more aspect of the fame of Jesus that requires our consideration is that the fame centered on Jesus. The news of what happened in the synagogue made neither the doctrine of deliverance nor any man famous. Nor did that particular synagogue building become an object of veneration or a pilgrimage spot. Rather the fame was about Jesus, His name, person, and ministry. It is only in this perspective that God gets glorified.

This is a lesson to many believers who have received a ministry of the miraculous, which often attracts publicity and fame. However, when this fame is mismanaged, it may lead to severely unfortunate consequences. Jesus set a perfect example in the way He handled His own fame. We will now consider three of the many scriptures that offer some guidelines about the attitude of Jesus to fame and glory:

- I do not receive glory from men" (John 5:41)
- "But I do not seek glory; there's one who seeks and judges" (John 8:50)
- "If I glorify myself, my glory is nothing; it is my Father who glorifies me" (John 8:54)

Most clearly, Jesus ascribed all the glory to the Father, who in turn glorified Jesus for all eternity. Jesus, being God, did humble Himself to a shameful death, but God exalted Him and gave Him a name above all names (Phil. 2:7–10). We, likewise, as the servants of Jesus do partake of the Lord's fame;

but we should not allow ourselves to be sidetracked by personal fame and glory. We must rather ascribe all glory to the Father through Jesus Christ, so that He will exalt us in due time. We must also make Jesus the focus of our lives; nothing else, including our ministry, or its success or failure, should be our focus. Our ultimate satisfaction should not be derived from anything apart from the conviction of our salvation and our ongoing solid relationship with the Lord Jesus Christ.

It is typically instructive for Christian ministers to recall the attitudes of the early disciples whom Jesus sent out in Luke 10:17–20. When they returned and were giving reports of their evangelism to the Lord, they were obviously excited to observe that the demons were subject to them. The Lord's response was that they should not rejoice in that but to rejoice in the fact that their names had been written in the book of life in heaven. I do not believe that the Lord rebuked them for their testimony. He indeed expected and did accept their testimony, but He was emphasizing the priority of personal salvation and the continual walk of personal fellowship of every believer with the Lord. When this priority is ignored, the unfortunate and tragic situation occurs whereby some who work healings and deliverance in the Lord's name are rejected and turned away from His presence on the last day.

There is no gainsaying the fact that many believers have received ministry gifts from God characterized by regular manifestation of the miraculous with a tremendous potential for power, fame, money and other forms of material rewards. However, we must resist the temptation to use these trappings for personal aggrandizement and instead glorify the Lord, focus on Him and publicize Him. Let us lift Him up so that He might continue to draw others and us unto Himself.

3

DELIVERANCE IN THE
MINISTRY OF JESUS

A
S FAR AS ministry is concerned, the ministry of Jesus is God's benchmark. No person in human history can lay claim to any kind of service to God that can compare with the ministry that Jesus the Son rendered to God the Father by the Holy Spirit. God's servants in the Old Testament were called to primarily foreshadow or foretell the unique ministry that God had anointed Jesus to fulfill in the fullness of time. Likewise, all of God's servants in the New Testament, beginning from the early church till the end of the age, are called not to develop new ministries or standards of ministry but to build on the ministry of Jesus. Thus, the ministry of the Lord Jesus is God's solid foundation for all present and future ministries called to the service of God and God's people.

Human involvement in Christian ministry is only a manifestation of God's grace, the endowment of a human vessel with the power of God to do something that only God can do. The only person who is qualified on the basis of His own personal merits to do ministry for God is Jesus. But out of His love and grace, He invites and shares His ministry with redeemed humanity. This vision of grace was not fully grasped by believers in Corinth to the extent that the apostle Paul had to sternly address this shortsightedness (1 Cor. 3:1–10). In fact, in 1 Corinthians 3:11 Paul dealt a blow to their carnality when he wrote, "For no one can lay a foundation, other than the one which is laid, which is Jesus Christ."

The Lord Jesus Christ is indeed God's Foundation, and God never hesitated to testify or attest to this at every critical point in His earthly life and ministry. Let us just consider one such incident, which occurred at the Transfiguration. Jesus had just been transfigured before three of His apostles, Peter, James, and John, when two of the most outstanding prophets of the Old Testament, Moses and Elijah, appeared. Peter, basking in the excitement of the moment, suggested that three tabernacles be built, one each for Moses, Elijah, and Jesus. This would, of course, imply the building of the foundations of the law (Moses), the prophets (Elijah), and of grace and the kingdom (Jesus). It also indicates an equality of these three persons and ministries, which Peter thought was correct. However, God's response clearly defined the uniqueness and divinity of Jesus as His Son. Moreover, it set apart the ministry of Jesus as most pleasing to God, "This is my beloved, Son, with whom I am well pleased; listen to Him" (Matt. 17:5).

Notice that God had to interrupt Peter and overshadow all that were present with a bright cloud, which I believe to be a manifestation of the Holy Spirit. Furthermore, God's attestation about Jesus was made in the presence of an unusual audience, the combined gathering of Old and New Testament saints.

If, therefore, we want to understand God's purpose, plan and method for any form of biblical ministry, Jesus is our perfect, unchanging Pattern. The ministry of Jesus while He was on earth was both broad in its scope and deep in its intensity and degree.

Contemporary Christian ministry, therefore, should not depart in any way from the pattern and methods employed by the author and finisher of the Christian faith, the Lord Jesus Christ. Unfortunately, in numerous ministries and in many sections of professing Christendom, there have been grave departures from the ministry methods and patterns of Jesus. There are many possible factors that could lead to such fruitless departures. The most common are unbelief, dependence on the flesh or self, fear of man (the desire to be accepted by others), ignorance about the promises of God in His Word, and also pride. Interestingly, all these attitudes are motivated by demons.

No one can improve upon the ministry of Jesus. And since Jesus is the author and finisher of our faith, wisdom demands that we learn from Him and continue to use the blueprints He designed, tested, and proved in His earthly ministry. It was His lifestyle of obedience and desire to do God's will in His personal life and ministry that gained for Him God's approval, abiding presence, and supernatural attestation.

DELIVERANCE

The purpose of this chapter is not to explore the entire ministry of Jesus on earth but to identify the place, purpose, role and results of His ministry of deliverance as God's appointed Messiah or Christ. Undoubtedly, Jesus did various ministry activities such as teaching, preaching, and the working of miracles such as deliverance, healings, raising the dead, and the divine provision of material needs. Invariably, all these were done to accomplish God's purposes in peoples' lives. However, upon closer examination, the ministering of deliverance was central at least in two ways.

First, Jesus spent most of His public ministry time in dealing with demons: rebuking them and casting them out. Apart from the many specific or named individuals who received deliverance through the ministry of Jesus, there are also several places in the record of the New Testament where Jesus dealt with demons in the lives of groups or masses of people simultaneously.

Second, another fact that underscored the place of the ministry of deliverance in Jesus' campaigns is that He employed this ministry at the beginning of and continued with it through the entire course of His ministry. He never thought of backing off or modifying it. Towards the end of His earthly ministry, when some Pharisees sought to discourage Him from fulfilling His purpose of going to Jerusalem, they tendered an intimidation: "Herod is seeking to kill you." Jesus' answer was no less intimidating, not only to Herod but also to the demonic forces behind Herod's motive: "Tell that fox, behold, I cast out demons and perform cures today, tomorrow, and on the third day I reach my goal" (Luke 13:32).

This answer not only reflects the vital place that deliverance occupied in the Lord's ministry, it also reveals the fact that deliverance as a ministry strategy was given a continuing practical emphasis. Furthermore, there is a goal to which the Lord aims to arrive through the deliverance ministry.

THE PURPOSE OF DELIVERANCE

Everything the Lord Jesus did in ministry was purposeful. He always had fellowship with God the Father, and out of this relationship He got to know the Father's purposes and the strategies adopted by the Father to meet such needs. In John's Gospel, Jesus says, "The Son can do nothing of Himself, unless it is something He sees the Father doing" (John 5:19). In other words, when the Father initiates His purpose in heaven, Jesus the Son implements the purpose on earth. I believe this principle guided all of Jesus' ministry action and strategies.

One immediate purpose of God is to undo Satan's work of corruption in humanity that began in the Garden of Eden, and to restore us to our place of glory, authority, victory, prosperity, and dominion through fellowship with God in Christ. We can safely say that this was a major purpose of the ministry of deliverance as revealed in many verses in both the Old and New Testaments. John in his first epistle clearly indicates this purpose, "The Son of God (Jesus) appeared for this purpose, that He might destroy the works of the devil" (1 John 3:8). The appearing or manifesting of Jesus from divinity and eternity to humanity and time was not a random demonstration of God's counsel and miraculous power. It was a purposeful, sovereign act. The purpose was to destroy all the works of darkness being perpetrated by Satan and his forces.

Satan himself is also very purposeful and strategic. Jesus exposed Satan's purpose, saying, "The thief comes only to steal, and kill, and destroy" (John 10:10). This evil purpose expressed as stealing, killing, and destroying inspires and motivates all of Satan's forces to carry out diabolic activities against humanity. But within the same verse of scripture, God's glorious purpose for us in Christ is also revealed: "I (Jesus) have come, that they might have life and have it more abundantly."

The Lord Jesus also elaborated on these aspects of His deliverance ministry when He appropriated the prophecy of Isaiah concerning the coming Messiah and His ministry. On a visit to a synagogue in His hometown of Nazareth, on a Sabbath day, the book of the prophet Isaiah was handed to Jesus. In that context, he found where His purpose was expressed in the following words, "The spirit of the Lord is upon me, because He anointed me to preach the gospel to the poor. He has sent me to proclaim release to the captives and recovery of sight to the blind, to set free those who are downtrodden. To proclaim the favorable year of the Lord" (Luke 4:18–19).

Without commenting on the individual aspects of this purpose and mandate, I would say that this declaration in all its ramifications speaks of deliverance. This was of such importance that the Father by the Holy Spirit anointed Jesus in order to fulfill such a ministry. The purpose of Jesus' ministry is summarily reviewed by Peter after Jesus had ascended and poured out the Holy Spirit, "God anointed Him (Jesus of Nazareth) with the Holy Spirit and with power, and how He went about doing good and healing all who were oppressed by the devil, for God was with Him" (Acts 10:38).

In both passages of Luke 4:18–19 and Acts 10:38, there is a clear indication that Jesus was invested with the Holy Spirit and divine power for the purpose of deliverance. Acts 10:38 clearly indicates that Jesus dealt with those oppressed or bound by the devil. This mostly resulted in the practical manifestation of God's goodness and diverse provisions, especially healing of sicknesses and freedom from demonic bondage.

The Result of Deliverance

The results produced by the ministry of deliverance in the earthly work of Jesus were, to say the least, dramatic and immeasurable. Moreover, these were practical results that could not have been produced by any method or ministry strategy other than the ministry of deliverance. This does not only demonstrate the central role that deliverance has in the administration of God's grace. Jesus' comment on the wicked and skeptical attitude of the pharisees concerning His ministry of deliverance also reveals, among other things, a great deal about the inner workings of this ministry, "But if I cast out demons by the Spirit of God, then the kingdom of God has come upon you" (Matt. 12:28).

The first truth revealed in this verse of Scripture is that Jesus did expel demons by the power of the Holy Spirit. The only power strong enough to drive evil spirits away is the anointing of the Holy Spirit, God's sovereign Spirit. The deliverance ministry, therefore, always and inevitably sets up a conflict of spirits between God's eternally indomitable and triumphant Holy Spirit, manifesting as God's finger of power and judgment (Exodus 8:19 and Luke 11:20), and the unclean and evil spirits of Satan that the Lord Jesus defeated on the cross.

The second truth of practical emphasis is that through the ministry of deliverance, Satan's evil rule over human lives and situations, or the environment, is overthrown and terminated. This termination of Satan's dominion often implies the practical reversal of Adam's Fall, and also of the consequences of the Fall such as sin, sickness, oppression, death, shame, failure, and all other forms of bondage. Simultaneously, through the ministry of deliverance, the central result of Christ's victory—righteousness manifesting as divine impartation of life, health, glory, success, freedom from bondage, and victory over sin—is made available to humanity.

In the Matthew 12:29, the Lord Jesus also poses a revealing question, "Or how can anyone enter the strong man's house and carry off his property, unless he first binds the strong man? And then plunder his house." The opening words of this question, *"How can...,"* suggest that it is only through the ministry of deliverance and other aspects of spiritual warfare that one can cross into the enemy's "secure" territory and seize his ill-gotten goods, which were originally God's provision to humanity. The strongman mentioned here is Satan, who takes people captive. The overall effect of deliverance in this sense is not only the overthrow of the strong man, but the plundering of his entire estate: every device and tool he has used to keep humanity alienated from God and God's provisions of freedom, righteousness, health, life, prosperity, holiness, glory, and power. This is an awesome transaction, yet the climax is the dramatic and simultaneous establishment of God's kingdom over all those who until the time of deliverance were held captive under Satan's rule.

In the words of the apostle Paul, this is described as, "For He (God) delivered us from the domain of darkness and transferred us to the kingdom of His beloved Son" (Col. 1:13). This act is a translation, a carrying over of a person from one realm of dwelling (Satan's kingdom of darkness) to a different realm of dwelling (God's kingdom in Christ). But this translation that comes from deliverance is not an expectation of something in a dispensational future but is available at this present time. The kingdom of God is at hand through the ministry of deliverance. This translation is essentially spiritual and invisible but manifests in the material realm as freedom from sin and all forms of demonic bondage.

These results have a special connection to the ministry of deliverance as Jesus Himself reveals in many portions of the New Testament. In one instance He mandates the twelve apostles, "As you go, preach, saying the kingdom of God is at hand" (Matt. 10:7). This is His primary evangelistic message, which He also expects us to preach. When this simple message is preached, there are certain practical results that should manifest. Hence, in the next verse, He commands the disciples to "heal the sick, raise the dead, cleanse the lepers, cast out demons. Freely you received, freely give" (Matt. 10:8).

These ministry manifestations, when they operate by the Holy Spirit and in the name of the Lord, demonstrate the presence of God's kingdom in a life or situation. It is significant to note that the list of such manifestations could not be completed without the inclusion of the phrase "cast out demons." Moreover, the investing of such power was a free gift. Therefore, the apostles were expected to be purposefully lavish with the use of this power to bless humanity. If the church of this age will heed this mandate, we will regain a lot more of what Satan had stolen from us.

LET US GO AND PREACH

In the ministry of the Lord Jesus, preaching meant much more than sweet, religious sermons. Preaching was never used as a political tool to mobilize sociopolitical action. It was not a psychological technique to boost morale. It was neither a self-help tool, nor a motivational device. Preaching was a proclamation of the good news or gospel announcing the arrival of God's King, His kingdom, and the simultaneous overthrow of Satan and his kingdom. Preaching in the earthly ministry of Jesus and the ministry of the early church always declared God's willingness and power to forgive sins, save, deliver from demons, and heal the sick.

It also implies the manifest demonstration of the power of God through the Holy Spirit and the spoken word of God's grace. Preaching, in essence, is the "heralding" of the imminence of God's will to take over and bless humanity and the earth. It always reveals God's blessings for humanity, as well as His judgment in history and eternity for those who would not receive God's love and grace in Jesus Christ, God's appointed King and Judge.

The preaching of God's kingdom always makes the demand of repentance, through which God offers forgiveness. Forgiveness then opens the door to God's salvation and all the blessings of New Testament salvation, which include righteousness and eternal life, victory over sin, freedom from demons, healing of sicknesses, divine health, the exercise of God's authority on earth, and hope of eternity in heaven.

Whenever Jesus and the early disciples spoke of preaching the gospel of the kingdom, implicit in their reference was the proclamation of God's demonstrable works of mercy, power and grace in people. In that sense, preaching as proclamation is a conduit for the various aspects of salvation especially healing and deliverance; therefore, it is an important platform from which dominion over demons may be exercised. For instance, when Peter came to Jesus in the company of other believers shortly after Jesus had ministered to the crowd with healing and deliverance, Peter said, "Everyone is looking for you" (Mark 1:37). Obviously the people were looking for Jesus because they were in need of salvation, healing, and deliverance because the Lord replied, "Let us go somewhere else to the towns nearby, in order that I may preach there also, for that is what I came out for" (Mark 1:38).

From the people's expectation and the Lord's response to Peter, it is evident that both He and His disciples realized there was a great need for healing and deliverance not only in Capernaum and in its environs but also on a global level. Moreover, the Lord specifically referred to preaching as His core strategy for the totality of His liberating ministry.

In other words, when the truth of the gospel is proclaimed, it releases the blessings of salvation, including forgiveness of sins, healing of diseases, deliverance from demons, and other provision for meeting people's needs. These blessings are God's attestation to the truth of the gospel thus preached. The writer of the Book of Hebrews indicated this when he challenged the believers, "How shall we escape if we neglect so great a salvation?

After it was first spoken through the Lord, it was confirmed to us by those who heard, God also bearing witness with them, both by signs and wonders and by various miracles and by gifts of the Holy Spirit according to His own will" (Heb. 2:3–4).

We must note the fact that the "great salvation" from God was first spoken by the Lord and later confirmed by the Lord's disciples. In either case, God bore witness to the proclaimed word with signs, wonders, miracles, and the gifts of the Holy Spirit. And judging by the records of the New Testament, the Lord's earthly ministry essentially consists of the ministry of the Word through preaching (proclamation), teaching (expounding), and the demonstration of the power of the spoken word and of the Holy Spirit through the practical ministering of salvation through the casting out of demons, healing, and other kinds of miracles. This was the pattern of Jesus' ministry from place to place. He was deliberate about this and stuck to it. He not only expected to encounter demons, sin, and sickness, but was also always prepared and willing to deal with them without compromise.

I would at this point cite some instances in the Gospel records where the Lord did minister to people's needs through the proclaimed Word and also demonstrated its power by ministering deliverance and healing. Some of these incidents entail a great number of individual cases of deliverance and healings procured en masse.

- Matthew 4:23–25; 8:16; 10:1, 8
- Mark 1:32–34; 3:10–11; 6:12–13
- Luke 4:40–41; 6:17–19; 7:20–22; 8:1–2; 9:1–2

There were, however, other cases in which He provided healing without necessarily casting out demons. Some people do believe that in such cases, most probably demons are not directly responsible for those sicknesses.

- Matthew: 8:1–4; 5:13; 9:1–8, 18–26; 20:29–34
- Luke: 17:11–19
- John 5:1–15; 9:1–12

The Lord not only personally retained this pattern in His ministry, but when He sent out His disciples during His earthly ministry, He entrenched this pattern—namely, to proclaim the good news and demonstrate it. When He commissioned the twelve apostles for evangelistic outreach, His ministry objectives and priority to be fulfilled by these twelve apostles were clearly stated in the following passages of scripture:

> And having summoned his twelve disciples, He gave them authority over unclean spirits (demons) to cast them out and to heal every kind of sickness.
>
> —MATTHEW 10:1

> And He called the twelve together and gave them power and authority over all the demons and to heal diseases, and He sent them out to proclaim the kingdom of God and to perform healings.
>
> —LUKE 9:1–2

> And He appointed twelve that they might be with Him and that He might send them out to preach and to have authority to cast out demons.
>
> —MARK 3:14–15

Apparently, following the successful sending out and ministry of the twelve, Jesus later appointed seventy other disciples for outreach. Also, His mandate in terms of objective, task, and priority of ministry was the same as those He gave the first team of twelve, "The Lord appointed seventy others and sent them two by two ahead of Him to every city and place where He Himself was going to come" (Luke 10:1). To this team of seventy disciples, His mandate was, "And heal those in it (the city) who are sick and say to them the kingdom of God has come near to you" (Luke 10:9). When these disciples returned from their mission, they testified about one particularly practical result, "Lord, even the demons are subject to us in your name" (Luke 10:17). Concerning this testimony and their experience in the novel ministry of deliverance, the Lord explained, "Behold, I have given you authority to tread upon serpents and scorpions and over all the power of the enemy and nothing shall injure you" (Luke 10:19).

In summarizing the commission of these two batches of disciples, I would conclude that:

1. In each case the disciples' primary mandate was to proclaim the gospel of the kingdom of God. This is the essence of preaching.

2. Implicit in this mandate of gospel proclamation is the exercise of the supernatural power and grace of casting out demons, healing the sick, and raising the dead among other supernatural signs.

3. In each case it was this necessary empowerment of the disciples with the supernatural power to cast out demons, heal the sick, and obtain divine protection that made their proclamation effective and practical. The Lord was deliberate with this principle, since He would not send out anyone for evangelistic or apostolic ministry without first

investing such a one with power and authority over demons. Notice also that demons were implicated as the primary and notorious agents of Satan's wicked dominion over lives, and in so doing they hindered the establishing of God's kingdom over such lives.

The deliverance ministry, therefore, is a core, integral component of the gospel. And since the gospel is the proclamation of the reality of God's kingdom, any preaching that regularly negates or omits the core facets of deliverance and healing is incomplete, and below the standard set by the Lord Jesus Christ.

The Great Commission

The Great Commission refers to the mandate the Lord Jesus gave His disciples when He made the post-resurrection appearance to them. The exact wordings and aspects of that mandate were recorded in all four Gospels and the Book of Acts (Matt. 28:18–20; Mark 16:14–18; Luke 25:46–49; John 20:21–23; Acts 1:8). The highlights of this mandate are as follows.

First, it is based on the authority invested in the Lord Jesus by the Father through the Holy Spirit. Second, this investment of authority in Jesus was in recognition of His defeat of Satan and Satan's kingdom through His death and resurrection (Luke 24:26). Third, this authority is limitless. The sphere of its territorial influence spans over the heavens, the earth, and beneath the earth. In other words, when believers rightly exercise His authority, angels in heaven, principalities and powers in the heavenlies, humans and demons on earth, and demons beneath the earth submit to it.

Fourth, believers should, therefore, go forth into all the

world with the good news (gospel) and proclaim that God is asking us to repent of sin and believe in His Son Jesus in order to receive forgiveness of sins and subsequently be taught the divine principles of righteous living in His kingdom (Luke 24:47). Fifth, when we repent and believe, we are forgiven, saved, and we receive eternal life. Subsequently, we are baptized in water by immersion into the name of the Father, the Son, and the Holy Spirit. Sixth, after we repent, believe the gospel, and receive eternal life, God will endue us with the power of the Holy Spirit without which we could never fulfill the commission. Thereafter, we will exhibit the following supernatural signs, namely, "In My Name they shall cast out demons, they will speak with new tongues, they will pick up serpents, and if they drink any deadly poison, it shall not hurt them, they will lay hands on the sick and they shall recover" (Mark 16:17–18).

Seventh, this initial clothing with the Holy Spirit and with power will take place in Jerusalem following an initial waiting season. This waiting season ended with the advent of the Holy Spirit on the day of Pentecost. Subsequently, and up to the present time, all Christians are to go into all the world proclaiming the gospel of God's kingdom with divine, super-natural signs and wonders following.

Having identified some of the major highlights of the Great Commission, the next logical question would be how the early disciples responded to or interpreted the mandate. Personally, I believe that the Book of Acts and the Epistles provide suffi-cient facts about how these elements of the commission were fulfilled. Starting from Pentecost in Acts 2, all the facets were fulfilled.

Concerning casting out of demons, the Book of Acts docu-ments many incidents whereby the early disciples confronted demons and expelled them. In Acts 8:3–13, Philip the evangelist invaded the city of Samaria with the gospel of Jesus Christ and made a tremendous supernatural impact. In verse 7, it was reported that demons departed from many people as the message of the gospel was proclaimed; healing and miracles followed this. The impact of the deliverance and miracle ministry of Philip was so great that Simon, a certain occult practitioner who had bewitched the entire city with his magic arts (to the extent that they regarded him as a god), believed, was baptized, and continued in the new faith. Simon had simply come to terms with the reality of the superiority of Jesus Christ over Satan and his forces when he witnessed the pure demonstration of the Holy Spirit by Philip through the deliverance ministry.

The ministry of Paul the Apostle is another good example of the demonstration of the Great Commission by the early church, especially as it concerns the subject of casting out of demons. In the city of Philippi in the region of Macedonia, Paul encountered a slave girl who had a spirit of divination, and he cast the spirit out of the girl (Acts 16:12, 16–21). Furthermore, in the city of Ephesus, when Paul proclaimed the gospel, God released extraordinary miracles marked especially by healing and deliverance from demons (Acts 19:12). There are other instances in the New Testament as to the manifest demonstration of the power of the Holy Spirit over demons whenever the Name, power, and kingdom of Jesus Christ are proclaimed in the fulfillment of the Great Commission.

Moreover, modern believers who have given heed to the Great Commission and acted in simple obedience will testify that the same results obtained by Philip, Paul and other earlier disciples of Jesus Christ are obtainable in their own present day ministries. Since Jesus has neither amended nor revoked this Commission, any negligence of any of its original facet or aspect is tantamount to not just a great omission but also grave disobedience.

DAIMON

D EMONS ARE DISEMBODIED, unclean, and evil spirit persons. In New Testament Greek, the word *demon* is *daimon*, which is derived from another Greek word, *daimonion*. These words are used to describe idols or foreign deities. Demons are thus believed to be inferior deities that are usually under the dominion or control of a higher cadre of gods or deities, presumably principalities.

BAALZEBUB

Ultimately, demons are under the control of Satan, also called the devil, whom they serve. The Greek word from which Satan's New Testament name *devil* is derived is *diabolos*. In the English language, this means "evil." There is only one devil or Satan, but an innumerable number of demons or evil spirits. It is important for us to realize that Satan is a separate entity from demons or unclean spirits. This clarification has become very necessary since some English versions of the New Testament use the word *devils* for demons. Such a mistranslation has given rise to a great deal of ignorance and confusion about the identities of Satan and demons, their respective nature, and their relationship.

The relationship between Satan and demons, as well as an important aspect of the motive of demons, is brought out in the outrageous lie and accusation the scribes and Pharisees alleged against Jesus in the course of His own deliverance ministry. When the Pharisees heard about: Jesus casting out demons, they said, "This man casts out demons only by Beelzebub (or, Baalzebub) the ruler of the demons" (Matt. 12:24; see also Matt. 9:34; Mark 3:22; and Luke 11:15). This statement is clearly a blasphemy against the Holy Spirit and His ministry through Jesus—the unforgivable sin (Matt. 12:31–32). However, the full implication of the statement is very revealing.

First, Beelzebub is a heathen deity believed to be the lord or "prince" of spirits. More literally, in its Philistine origin, it is the "lord of flies." Interestingly, both the Pharisees and the Lord Jesus ascribed this title to Satan. In other words, the devil as a false god has rule or lordship over these unclean, dung-filled evil spirits. Everything that demons do, they do under the leading and power of Satan. It is for his diabolic purpose that demons unleash evil upon humanity.

The second implication of the blasphemous charge of the Pharisees against Jesus is that by referring to demons as flies, we are made aware of some similarities of nature between insects and demons. In other words, demons are spiritual flies or insects, yet another cadre of creeping things. As spiritual insects, they are capable of all the unsanitary and unhygienic properties of insects. They are indeed "disease vectors" capable of all sorts of harm and evil in both the spiritual and physical realms of life. Generally, demons are invisible spirit persons with supernatural abilities. However, they are not divine. They are absolutely evil, unclean, and depraved. On the contrary, the Holy Spirit is not only invisible and supernatural, but also divine.

PERSONALITY

Demons, like other spirit persons such as human spirits, angels, and the Holy Spirit, have the following attributes of personality:

- Personal identity, or self-awareness (Mark 5:9): Demons know who they are. They are aware of their personality
- Knowledge (Matt. 12:44; Acts 19:15): Demons are able to recognize other persons, things and places
- Speech (Matt. 12:44): Demons speak and communicate with other persons
- Emotion (James 2:19): Demons are capable of a wide range of emotional attitudes and reactions, including acknowledgement, shock, anger, surprise, and fear.
- Will (Matt. 12:44): Demons are capable of making decisions and following through on their decisions
- Activity (Matt. 12:43): Demons are not just active but capable of purposeful and destructive evil acts.

These attributes do not in anyway give credit to demons; however they are basic characteristics of any human or spiritual entities that are persons by nature.

ORIGINS

The next critical question that often attends any serious discussion on demons is the question of their origin. I believe that apart from earlier references to Satan and creeping things in the Book of Genesis, the Bible does not give any specific reference as to their origin. However, there are sufficient references to the origin of Satan himself and to some other categories of fallen beings. This has given room to a certain degree of controversy concerning what these beings were before they became demons.

Some Bible scholars and believers rest their case on this biblical counsel: "The secret things belong to the Lord our God: but the things revealed belong to us and our sons forever, that we may observe all the words of this law" (Deut. 29:29). In other words there is no one specific and direct scripture reference as to the origin of demons. Without getting involved in deep speculations, it may be helpful to observe that many Bible teachers and believers build upon one or more of the following theories. In any case, these theories offer only probable explanations for the origin of demons.

- Demons are offspring of the unnatural cohabiting between certain rebellious angels and some earthly women in the antediluvian age or time of Noah (Gen. 6:1–6).

- Demons are fallen angels who rebelled with Satan against God before creation. Proponents of this view usually cite Psalm 78:49, Jude 6:2, Peter 2:4, and Ephesians 6:12 to buttress their position. This view maintains that when these angels fell, they became demons and began harassing humans.

- Demons are pre-Adamic spirits that are not angels at all but have a different form of life. Proponents primarily believe that demons are spirits of disembodied beings of the age that existed before Adam was created. The major scriptural impetus used by these proponents is found in Genesis 1:1–2, which supports the argument that an unmeasured period of time did exist between the first two verses of the first chapter of Genesis. In this perspective, verse one is believed to be a description of the prior age, which was created perfect. The second verse is believed to describe the judgment that came upon that prior age and the subsequent creation of the "Adamic age." In other words, the first verse addressed the existence of a pre-Adamic race, which existed for ages and supposedly came under judgment on account of Lucifer's fall. The judgment, it is claimed, rendered the earth without form and made it void. (Gen 1:2) It was, therefore, out of this situation of utter devastation that almighty God created a new earth and a new race—"Adam's race." Part of the judgment was the stripping of the pre-Adamic beings of their bodies and subjecting their spirits to creeping, as well as a destiny in the abyss.

This theory also holds that humanity was not always subject to demons. Humans were, in fact, given dominion over them. However, we became subject to them through the Fall of Adam and Eve (Gen. 1:12; Jer. 4:23). In addition to these scriptures listed above, and again without getting too deep into this theory, the major scriptural plank used by its proponents is found in Isaiah 45:18, "For thus saith the LORD that created the heavens; God Himself that formed the earth and made it; He hath established it, He created it not in vain, He formed it to be inhabited; I am the Lord; and there is none else."

It may be deduced from this passage that the earth in Genesis 1:1 was not created in vain. In other words the waste, void, and devastation portrayed in verse 2 of Genesis 1 were the result of judgment upon the earth of verse 1. It is believed that the earth of verse 1 was the earth that existed before Adam was brought into being—the pre-Adamic age when Lucifer prominently ministered before God. The earth of verse 2 portrays Lucifer's fall and consequent judgment. The earth of verses 2 and 3 is the new earth created for Adam and his race before his own Fall in Genesis 3. The argument of this theory, therefore, is that demons are the spirits of the rebellious inhabitants of the earth of Genesis 1:2 who re-entered and invaded the earth by reason of the Fall. This is only one of the many theories about the origin of demons deduced from the Bible.

Another common argument has to do with whether demons and fallen angels are the same kind of beings. Many scholars believe that demons are different from fallen angels. So, the follow up question is this: if demons are not fallen angels, then what is the difference between the two? There are, for our present purposes, at least two scripturally deduced points commonly used to differentiate demons from fallen angels. One, fallen angels essentially are airborne and mostly fly or operate in the heavenly realms and close to the surface of the earth; hence, Satan is called the prince of the power of the air, while demons are essentially earthbound and mostly walk in dry places on the earth (Matt. 12:43; Eph. 2:2). It is possible, therefore, to infer that fallen angels have spiritual bodies and wings, whereas demons are disembodied. Two, fallen angels are mostly territorial in their operation. They are the particular agents of Satan's kingdom implicated as the prince and kings of Persia and Greece in Daniel 10:12–13 and 20, and the various invisible Satanic forces implicated in Acts 19:23–29 and Ephesians 6:12. On the other hand, demons indwell and trouble individual victims. In the case of fallen angels or principalities and other similar satanic agents, one principality dominates over whole families, communities, tribes, municipalities, people groups, and nations. These usually control their victims from outside the human body. This satanic strategy is profusely revealed in God's Word, but one of the most precise mentions is in the prophecy of Zechariah 1:21, "These are the horns which have scattered Judah so that no man lifts up his head."

In any case it is more important for us to remember that Satan, as a fallen angel, rules over a host of evil, rebellious kingdom of beings including:

- Other fallen angels who are now mostly referred to as principalities, powers, and the spiritual forces of wickedness in heavenly places;
- Demons: evil, unclean spirits whose main goal is to indwell and trouble humans on earth;
- Human servants of Satan who completely yield to Satan and are manipulated by principalities and demons to inflict harm to humanity, especially God's people and God's purpose. These include such Bible characters such as Cain, Pharaoh and his magicians, Janis and Jambres, Baalak, Baalam, Jezebel, Simon of Samaria, and the slave girl of Philippi.

I believe that demons are different from fallen angels; however, both of them are equally evil, wicked spiritual servants of Satan sent against humanity. And since it is not within the scope of this book to explore more fully the activities of all of Satan's servants, we shall continue to focus on the activities of demons and their ultimate defeat in the name and authority of the Lord Jesus Christ. However, I must not fail to point out that when the Lord defeated Satan, it was not only Satan but all his forces—fallen angels, demons, and his human servants—that were defeated, overthrown, and stripped of their powers.

Habitat

Another important fact about demons that needs to be exposed is their residence. Knowledge about where demons live and thrive equips the believer with a clearer and better strategy to deal with them. Undoubtedly, the Bible sufficiently deals with the subject of their residence. A more comprehensive treatment of this subject is found in the Gospels:

> Now when the unclean spirit goes out of a man it passes through waterless places, seeking rest and does not find it. Then it says, "I will return to my house from which I came," and when it comes, it finds it unoccupied, swept and put in order. Then it goes and takes along with it seven other spirits more wicked than itself and they go in and live there and the last state of that man becomes worse than the first.
>
> —Matthew 12:43–45

Another illumination on this subject is given in the case of the Gadarene demoniac as recorded in Matthew 8:28–35, Mark 5:1–24, and Luke 8:26–37. When Jesus confronted the legion of demons that had possessed the man, their plea revealed much about their habitat. The passage in Matthew's Gospel reads, "If you are going to cast us out, send us into the heard of swine"

(8:31). Mark's Gospel reveals that the demons entreated the Lord not to send them into the country (5:10). Further down the passage, the demons request, "Send us into the swine so that we may enter them" (5:12). In Luke's account, the demons' primary entreaty was not to be "commanded to depart into the abyss" (8:31). Furthermore, they also sought permission to enter the swine (8:32). These passages clearly reveal at least four general places of residence for demons.

1. "My House"

In Matthew 12:44, Jesus exposed the arrogant attitude and false claim of demons concerning the human body. Demons consider the human body as their house. Apparently, this claim originates from the Fall of Adam. Going by the pre-Adamic origin theory, demons were not always disembodied beings. They probably became disembodied as a result of the judgment that came upon their pre-Adamic earth. Subsequently, against their will and convenience, these beings were subjected to live outside a body. Moreover, as a result of Adam's Fall, the human race became subject to demonic oppression and control.

Resultantly, demons began to gain access into and indwell the human body. After the Fall, demons found it a most comfortable accommodation and environment. As long as the body of their victim is conducive to them, they find rest and nurture and thus work out their unclean, evil, and wicked purposes in and through that body and against other people. Sin, sickness, corruption, failure, and oppression are the outcome of their uninterrupted occupation of a human body.

In the new creation through the death and resurrection of the Lord Jesus Christ, the claim of demons over the human body as their house is no longer valid. If the believer in Jesus Christ continually yields his or her body to the Holy Spirit, evil spirits will have no place in such bodies because in Christ, the believer's body is the temple of the Holy Spirit. (They may taunt from the outside but not dwell within the believer's Holy Spirit-filled body.) This is part of God's plan of salvation in Christ Jesus. Conversely, the body of the unbeliever remains under the claim of demons. However, through repentance and faith in Jesus Christ, such demonic claim can be revoked through a valid deliverance ministry. As long as the believer yields his or her body to the Lord, demons will not gain access. Even if they do, they will be expelled in the name of the Lord. If the believer ceases to yield to the Holy Spirit, he or she may give demons access they should not have.

2. Dry Places

Another common dwelling place for demons is known as "dry places" (Matt. 12:43; Luke 11:24, 1); some other versions call it "waterless places" or wilderness. As I understand it, dry places include any place outside the human or organic body. It also extends to the abyss (see Luke 8:31).

The main features of dry places were described in Matthew 12:43, "When the unclean spirit goes out of a man, it passes through waterless places, seeking rest and does not find it." In other words, the first place demons go to when they are cast out of a human body is outside the body. As far as demons are concerned, there is a great world of difference between being in the human body and out of the human body. In the body, they readily find comfort, peace, and rest. Outside the body, they go on "seeking rest and findeth none" (Matt. 12:43).

As long as demons remain in these dry places, they will undergo unending torment. They experience a harsh, unfavorable, wilderness environment. My picture of this condition is akin in many ways to that of a human being thrust out of a house into an unsheltered climate without appropriate clothing or advance notice. The only logical and lifesaving option is for that person to seek to force himself or herself into anything that can readily provide some form of shelter. Likewise, when demons are forced out of the body, they readily make a decision to force themselves back into their former habitat or victim. They are daring at this, so much that they seek full reinforcement by enlisting more demons (Matt. 12:45). If they fail to re-enter their former victim, they will seek out another vulnerable person to indwell since they must inhabit a body.

3. Swine

In the case of the Gadarene demoniac, a third possible habitat was revealed as swine. In the Gospels, the demons not only sought the Lord's permission to enter the swine, they actually did so.

The bodies of the swine were clearly preferred to the dry places because they provided something close to what the human body would provide. Swine are not the only animals that can provide a habitat or sanctuary for demons. Other animals, especially cats, dogs, snakes, and cows, are often demonized. There are innumerable accounts of demons operating through animals in accomplishing Satan's purposes in the lives of people. I am led to share this highly reported case. This story did not only make it to the evening news of most television networks and the pages of many big city newspapers, but was first reported in the reputable *New England Journal of Medicine*.[1] This was a case of a two-year-old cat in a dementia unit of a nursing home, which was noted to have negatively influenced the prognosis of dying patients. It was observed that in twenty-five cases, when this cat lay next to such a patient, the patient died within four hours. Although some medical minds think there is a biochemical basis for this strange phenomenon, I believe this is a classic case of a demon (or spirit) of death operating through the cat. This does not suggest that every cat or animal is demon possessed, but they are often vulnerable to demonic possession.

4. Abyss

The abyss is the prison for the confinement of demons. It is a deep pit reserved for a predetermined judgment on demons in time. It is also referred to as the "deep" (Rom 10:7; Rev. 9:1; 20:1–3) or a bottomless pit. The abyss is basically infernal in outlook; hence demons detest going there.

> And they were entreating Him not to command them to depart into the abyss.
>
> —Luke 8:31

5

BROKEN BORDERS: PART I
How Demons Enter the Human Personality

====================

A HUMAN PERSONALITY IS a spirit, possessing a soul and a tabernacle the human body. In creation, God first made a body of clay and breathed into that body His breath—the Spirit and life of God—and a living soul emerged (Gen. 2:7). The soul is the living being called man, or a person. The soul is, therefore, a product of the union between the body of clay and the breath (the Spirit) of almighty God.

Originally, the resulting soul or "being" was a partaker of the divine life of God. In fact, this life was the very image and nature of God. Since it was the perfect image and likeness of God, without corruption and blemish, God made it His personal representative on earth. Humans had complete dominion over everything that God had made. Unfortunately, when we sinned, we died spiritually and our bodies became corrupt and subject to all forms of evil influences such as disease and demonic attacks. Our spirits were cut off from fellowship with God, resulting in spiritual death (Eph. 2:1–5).

God's purpose for the human body is possession by the Holy Spirit as an incorruptible temple, a living sacrifice unto God (Rom. 12:1). The human body in this condition becomes a vessel in God's hands for the fulfillment of His purposes. Unfortunately, Adam's Fall produced many negative effects on this body, which can be summed up in one word: *corruption*.

The commonest manifestations of corruption in the body are sickness (or disease), weakness, and degeneration.

On the cross, the Lord Jesus redeemed humanity from the power of the enemy. This redemption on the cross was further validated by His triumphant resurrection whereby He imparts a new kind of life—the resurrection life—to all who believe in Him. So at this present time, although the believer has a resurrection life, his or her body is still a mortal body. This mortal body, if yielded to the Holy Spirit, is continually nourished, renewed, quickened, or healed with the resurrected life of Jesus within the believer as released by the indwelling Holy Spirit. The apostle Paul addressed this question in his Epistle to the believers in Rome in the following words, "But if the spirit of Him who raised Jesus from the dead dwells in you, He who raised Christ Jesus from the dead will also give life (quicken) your mortal bodies through His Spirit who indwells you" (Rom. 8:11). To those in Corinth, Paul referred to this divine operation as "the life of Jesus...made manifest in our mortal flesh" (2 Cor. 4:11). The final and complete effects of Christ's redemption on the human body will be made manifest at the future resurrection and rapture of the saints. On that occasion and in an instant, Jesus the Son of God will through the Holy Spirit transform the believer's body from mortal to immortal, corrupt to incorrupt, and shameful to glorious. This mystery is the subject of 1 Corinthians 15:51–57 and Philippians 3:20–21.

This glorious event will mark the final outworking of the defeat of Satan, sin, death, demons, disease, and all other aspects of corruption. It is our choice, therefore, to yield our body to the Lord or to Satan; and if we yield our body to the Lord, the Holy Spirit takes over full possession and control of it. Only then shall we serve the Lord with our body. Conversely, if we yield our body to Satan or to unrighteousness, then demons or evil spirits will take control to fulfill Satan's evil purposes in and through the body. The basic principle behind the operation of demons in the human body is exposed in this scripture, "Do you not know that when you present yourselves to someone as slaves for obedience, you are slaves of the one whom you obey, either of sin resulting in death or of obedience resulting in righteousness?" (Rom. 6:16).

When we yield or present any part of our body to Satan, we become enslaved and thereafter are compelled to obey him, leading to more corruption, decay, and death.

A Spiritual Wall

Almighty God in His marvelous wisdom has fashioned the human body beautifully and fenced it with a wall of protection. Within the body, apart from the physical cells, tissues and other organic components is the spirit—the human spirit. This spirit was cut off from God and died at the Fall, but it was regenerated at redemption through the death and resurrection of the Lord Jesus Christ. Moreover, the human spirit could be yielded to either the Holy Spirit or evil spirits. Ultimately, pending the Day of Judgment, God permits every person the control of his or her own body and spirit, "He who is slow to anger is better than the mighty, and be who rules his spirit than he who captures a City" (Prov. 16:32).

What a tremendous responsibility to have rule over one's spirit! To do this effectively entails keeping it in a stable state and guarding against infiltration, contamination, and corruption. When a human being lets go of this control over his or her spirit for any reason, the wall of spiritual protection is broken and the result is a massive invasion and bombardment of the inner person by unclean spirits and evil influences. Concerning this, the Bible says, "Like a city that is broken into and without walls is a man who has no control over his spirit" (Prov. 25:28).

For the most part, the protective wall God built around the spirit and the body is compromised by negative attitudes and self-destructive habits and lifestyles. When these walls or hedges are broken, there is a tendency for negative or evil forces and influences to harm those thus unprotected. The divine principle behind this is reiterated in the following passage of Scripture, "He who digs a pit may fall into it, and a Serpent may bite him who breaks through a wall" (Eccl. 10:8).

Satan and his evil forces are not only aware of the power of God's wall of protection around His people, but they also know from experience its divine efficacy. In the case of God's servant Job, the following dialogue between God and Satan over Job's condition has been revealed as a lesson to us:

> And the Lord said to Satan, "Have you considered my servant Job? For there is no one like him on the earth, a blameless and upright man fearing God and turning away from evil." Then Satan answered the Lord. "Does job fear God for nothing? Hast thou not made a hedge about him and his house and all that he has, on every side? Thou hast blessed the work of his hand and his possessions have increased in the land. But put forth thy hand now and touch all that he has; he will surely curse thee to thy face." Then the Lord said to Satan, `Behold, all he has is in your power, only do not put forth your hand on him." So Satan departed from the presence of the Lord.
>
> —Job 1:8–12

We see in the case of Job that Satan had previously been shut out of Job's life by God's impenetrable wall of defense. This wall is physically invisible, made up of God's angelic forces and the fire of the Holy Spirit, as revealed in the case of the prophet Elisha.

I personally can testify to this in my own life and ministry. One particular case in my own experience readily comes to mind. Many years ago while I was living in Benin City in midwestern Nigeria, I had just come into the ministry of deliverance. One evening as I was speaking on the subject of spiritual warfare during a midweek prayer meeting and deliverance service, I had just begun to confront and assail Satan with scriptures when suddenly a young woman in the audience who needed deliverance from demons bolted out of the meeting. However, she was brought back, and at the end of the meeting as she was being ministered to she revealed to me the demonic plot she witnessed while I was preaching. She said the demons tried to attack me on the platform, but they could not penetrate a wall of fire that surrounded me. They turned to her and that was why she abruptly left the meeting. A few weeks later, I found the following words in the Bible: "For I, declares the Lord, will be a wall of fire around her, and I will be the glory in her midst" (Zech. 2:5). What a mighty God we serve, who in His sovereignty aborts all satanic and demonic plots against us!

Having considered this much about the basic structure, composition, and operation of the human personality and the basic premise for infiltration and attack by evil influences, let us proceed to explore in more specific ways some portals of entry and modes of operation of demons into the human body. The list we are about to explore now is by no means exhaustive, and the phrases used may be unfamiliar to the reader; but I trust that the experiences described may be familiar and helpful in some way where they are apt.

1. Involvement in Cults and False Religions

False religions are all non-Christian religions. In other words, any religion that denies that Jesus Christ is the Son of God, and the only way to God, is a false religion. False religions also refuse to accept the atoning death of Jesus Christ on the cross, His burial, and His resurrection from death as the only basis for the salvation of humanity (Rom. 4:25; 10:9–10). The rejection of the above realities and the reliance on other sources for salvation constitutes idolatry. Generally, false religions and cults covertly or overtly deny or reject one or more of the fundamental tenets of biblical Christianity. Such tenets include but are not limited to:

- Godhead or Trinity (Deut. 6:4; Matt. 3:13–17; 28:19; 2 Cor. 13:14; Col. 2:9)
- Deity of Jesus Christ (Isa. 9:6–7; John 1:1; 8:58; 20:28)
- Virgin birth of Jesus Christ (Isa. 7:14; 9:6–7; Matt. 1:18–25; Luke 1:25–36)
- Atoning death of Jesus Christ on the cross of Calvary (Matt. 27:27–56; 1 Cor. 15:3–4)
- Bodily resurrection of Jesus Christ from death (Matt. 28:115; Luke 24:39; 1 Cor. 15:4)
- Salvation solely by means of God's grace and only through personal faith in the Lord and Savior Jesus Christ (Rom. 10:13; Gal. 3:22; Eph. 2:8)
- Ascension of Jesus to God's right hand in heaven (Acts 1:9; Heb. 1:3)
- Future personal return of the Lord Jesus Christ to earth and to rule in His kingdom (Acts 1:11; 1 Thess. 4:6–18)

Personal or family involvement in groups that reject or deny these teachings brings such individuals or groups into a covenant with Satan. On the basis of such covenants, these people are opened up to all sorts of evil influences, including demonic activities. These demons are the spirits behind all false gods or idols (1 Cor. 10:19–21).

We must bear in mind that Scripture tells of only one true God whose name is Jehovah-Elohim, and whose only Mediator with humanity is His only begotten Son the Lord and Savior Jesus Christ.

> Is it not I, the Lord? And there is no other God besides me, (Jehovah-Elohim), a righteous God and a savior; there is none except me.
> —ISAIAH 45:21

> For there is one God and one mediator between God and man, the man Christ Jesus.
> —1 TIMOTHY 2:5

If Jehovah-Elohim is the only true God, then all other so-called gods are idols corruptly empowered by evil spirits, also known as demons.

Essentially, any denial of Jehovah's claim as the only true God or the acceptance of any other gods is idol worshiping. Often, idolatry involves worshiping a multiplicity of gods especially through the use of carved images, fetishes, animals, trees and other natural objects, or entities in the created universe such as the sun, the moon, bodies of water, and people (Rom. 1:20–23). It also usually involves a set of rituals. However, a more subtle form of idolatry most common in western societies and even within professing Christendom involves the devoting of glory, honor, talent, time, and effort (due only to God) to carnal appetites and all forms of value systems such as entertainment, career, or food and drink (Phil. 3:19).

Ultimately, idolatry seeks to rob the Creator of His glory (Rom. 1:18–25). When idolatry is introduced into a family, it runs its evil course through future generations. Such evil inheritance sustains a historical pattern of negative family incidents and experiences, such as genetic defects, hereditary or chronic illnesses, marital failures, premature death, mental illness and disability, suicide, addictions, unfruitfulness, barrenness, and sexual pervasions, especially incest, adulteries, teenage pregnancies and other forms of illicit sexual activities. Other forms of attendant curses include poverty, a pattern of personal frustration and failures in life endeavors, accident proneness, and many other repetitive patterns of family tragedies and mishaps. Behind each of these experiences and conditions is a demon, which has exploited an open door granted to it by idolatry.

Usually, the contact point is an ancestor, a late or living grandparent, an immediate parent, an uncle, aunt, or sibling, or the individual involved in a non-Christian religion, cult, or secret society such as freemasonry and other forms of lodges. There are also cults of Christendom, which are sects or groups that profess to be a part of Christianity yet deny the basic biblical tenets of Christianity as enumerated above.

In any case, God's attitude toward idolatry is clear. He visits such historical iniquity of the father on the children up to the third and fourth generation (Exod. 20:1–5). When God's wrath is thus released against such persons, families or groups, His divine protection is withdrawn. Demons in turn harass, torture, and dominate such persons and families.

The only power strong enough to terminate demonic dominion and the curse of idolatry is the power of the gospel of the Lord Jesus Christ, "Christ redeemed us from the curse of the law, having become a curse for us—for it is written, cursed is everyone who hangs on a tree—in order that in Christ Jesus the blessing of Abraham might come to the Gentiles, so that we might receive the promise of the Spirit through faith" (Gal. 3:13–14).

On the cross of Calvary, Jesus became a curse by taking the curse reserved for humanity upon Himself so that any individual or family who believes in Him might receive God's favor and blessing through the Holy Spirit. In other words, the power of the blood of Jesus Christ revokes the evil covenant and ushers in the New Covenant; a covenant of forgiveness, mercy, life, and prosperity. This grace is only received when. Jesus Christ is received by faith as Lord and Savior.

2. Involvement in the occult

The occult is a branch or form of idolatry. In order not to confuse the words *cult* and *occult*, I would suggest that while the word *cult* refers to some form of false religious group, the term *occult* refers to certain deceptive religious practices or rituals. Most cults indulge in a variety of occult practices in their worship of false gods.

The word *occult* simply means "secret" or "hidden." In other words, the real nature of occult practices is "covered over" and the actual workings of occult practices are covered up in much secrecy and mystery. Outwardly, however, the effects or results of such practices are not only manifest, but dramatic and in many cases fascinating.

It is this fascination that draws people into occultism in the way a harlot would entice a young man into immorality. In fact, idolatry, including occultism, is considered in the Bible as spiritual adultery (Prov. 5:3–6; Hosea 4:12).

The primary motivations behind occultism are the quest for supernatural knowledge usually through fortune telling (divination) and the quest for supernatural power through witchcraft and sorcery. A breakdown of the overall picture of occultism brings out the individual, ancient practices still in use in most of our modern society for the acquisition of supernatural power and knowledge, some of which are:

- astrology (stargazing)
- charming (use of charms)
- divination (fortune telling, clairvoyance, clairaudience, palm reading, psychics, horoscopes, crystal ball reading)
- enchantment (chants and incantations employed by witches, wizards, magicians, animists and other human servants of Satan. Chants and incantations are also used in some forms of modern music such as rock, disco, rap, and aspects of reggae.)
- familiar spirits (through the use of mediums, séances and consulting of demons) observing of times (horoscopy, monthly prognostication)
- necromancy (consulting the spirits of the dead)
- witchcraft (various forms of contemporary spiritual practices with roots in ancient witchcraft)
- sorcery (a branch of occultism that entails a heavy dependence on objects believed to possess some form of supernatural power. Certainly, these objects are infested with demons and are accursed and fetish. Some examples include ankhs, special rings or finger bands, especially those used for covenants, birthstones, crystal balls, lucky symbols, special bracelets, hex signs,

inverted horseshoes, "holy water," religious scap-
ulars, and idolized images, pictures or carved
images of religious figures, leaders, or gurus.)

- occult literature (magazines, newspapers, peri-
odicals and books dedicated for the propagation,
promotion, and advancement of cults and occult
philosophies and practices)

- observing of days (mystery or jinx dates, days
and events). One of the simplest ways through
which millions of people become enslaved by
demons is by their submission to a list of certain
"dos" and "don'ts" on certain mystery days or
dates such as Friday the 13. In other cases, the
victims are ensnared into accepting a potential
for or an actual pattern or cycle of misfortune
or mishap if a certain normal activity or the use
of certain personal articles is or is not undertaken on certain days or seasons. For example,
some people associate wearing of a certain color
to misfortunes, such as failure in a test or job
interview. Other similar outcomes—accidents,
sickness, and death—are also associated with
such choices. Usually, such victims live with
some form of "jinx" mentality that opens a wide
door for demons into their lives. The Bible's
alternative mentality is that Jesus Christ through
His death and resurrection had rendered powerless Satan and all his forces so that Jesus "might
deliver those who through fear of death were
subject to slavery all their lives" (Heb. 2:15).

There are hundreds of thousands of other occult practices in use all over the world, including color therapy, omens, séances or mediums, tarot cards, handwriting analysis, iridology, mind reading, kabala, numerology, phrenology, telepathy, Ouija boards, dream analysis, extra sensory perception (ESP), and others. Occult practitioners and those who patronize them seek to obtain supernatural knowledge, revelation, and power with which to dominate or control nature, institutions, authorities, other individuals, and ultimately mankind. The folly of such evil, selfish, inordinate craving is the attempt to reach God without going through the God—ordained initiative of the Holy Spirit and the cornerstone mediation of the Lord Jesus Christ.

Such wisdom on their part is not only sensual, but demonic in its origin. Here is the Bible's estimation of such wisdom, "This wisdom is not that which comes down from above, but is earthly, natural (carnal), and demonic" (James 3:15).

Any attempt to circumvent the Lord Jesus Christ and the Holy Spirit in search of access to almighty God for supernatural revelation and power is illegitimate and will always expose such practitioners to demonic contact and control. Invariably, such practitioners will acquire some form of fake, corrupt, evil revelation, and power. Needless to say, such revelation and power, though supernatural, is not divine because the source is satanic. Every supernatural gift from God is given in Christ Jesus by the anointing of the Holy Spirit. The gifts and spiritual experiences from Jesus through the Holy Spirit are not only supernatural, but also divine and pure. They are never corrupt. God's prescription for seeking genuine supernatural religious or spiritual experience is clearly stated:

> For through Him (Jesus Christ) we both have our access in one Spirit to the Father.
> —Ephesians 2:18

On the other hand, demonic supernatural gifts and experiences bring their seekers and practitioners under bondage. Through occult practices, people enter into a pact with Satan, who dominates them through his demons. Hence God's Word says, "The thief cometh not, but for to steal, and to kill and to destroy. I (Jesus) came that they may have life and have it more abundantly" (John 10:10). Jesus precisely describes the personal and family destiny—theft, murder, and destruction—of those who surrender to such hireling occult practitioners. The actual nature of personal and family bondage associated with occultism is similar to those at work in false religion. God severely detests occultism in all its forms, and a careful study of Scripture reveals in detail the nature and forms of occultism, the destiny of occult practitioners, and God's attitude towards them (Deut. 4:19; 18:9–14; Isa. 47:12–15; Jer. 10:26; Dan. 2:24–28; Acts 19:9–11; 13:6–12).

The vanity of occultism is exposed in three main ways:

First, predictions and some other claims of occultism mostly turn out to be false and unfulfilled (Deut. 18:20–22). Second, in some cases, they are fulfilled; but so long as they are not in consonance with the Word of God; there is no life in them (Isa. 8:20). Third, because they have no life in them, they lead people to rebel against Jehovah and His anointed, Jesus Christ (Lev. 20:6–8; Isa. 8:18–20).

The truth is that the most simple, "entertaining," and seemingly innocuous brand of occultism is evil before God, and destructive and dangerous to us. Unfortunately, occultism is a rapidly growing phenomenon and from its very beginnings has always fascinated unguarded minds.

Finally, the good news is that God is willing to deliver any individual or family who has in any way been exposed to occultism and idolatry in the past or present. And for this purpose almighty God demands this, "'Therefore, come out from their midst and be separate,' says the Lord, 'And do not touch what is unclean and I will welcome you and I will be a Father to you and you shall be sons and daughters to me' says the Lord Almighty" (2 Cor. 6:17–18).

If you would respond to these promises right now, repent, denounce occultism, and renounce your involvement, then invite the Lord Jesus Christ into your life and family. He will save you instantly and begin to reveal God's destiny for you and your family.

3. Religious seduction

Millions of religious people are misled by demons into wrong doctrines and heresies. Through such, many sincere religious people are drawn away from biblically revealed truth into corrupted truth and sometimes outright error. History is full of accounts and incidents of groups or entire religious movements that were led astray, sometimes with tragic results. Common examples of such demonically inspired errors are the use of vegetarianism and other forms of religious food laws as a means of achieving righteousness; mass celibacy, and certain strange rules guiding relationship between spouses; extreme apocalyptic preoccupation and doomsday prophesying; intentional mass suicides; submission to religious commune-based lifestyles; polygamy; and submission to certain "charismatic" persons or leaders who claim and receive "messianic" status from their followers. Religious or spiritual domination, manipulation, and mass immorality are other features of seduction. Some of these seductions are found among the "cults of Christendom" mentioned before; certain groups that associate themselves with professing Christendom, but reject the basic tenets of the church. The real essence of religious seduction is revealed in the fact that some of these groups were like the

Galatian church. They began in truth, but got "bewitched" or brought under the power of witchcraft and thereafter slid into legalism and carnality (Gal. 3:1-3; 4:8-11; 1 Tim. 4:1-7; 2 Pet. 2:1-2; 1 John 4:1-3, 6).

The real forces at work here are exposed in 1 Timothy 4:1-7 where Paul, speaking by the Holy Spirit—the Spirit of truth—refers to this trend as a "falling away from the truth." This spiritual condition is known as apostasy and is orchestrated by doctrines of demons. This simply reveals the fact that all false doctrines peddled in churches and other religious circles are inspired by demons. These demonically inspired doctrines are deceptive and entice or seduce people into error. These demons gain access to any person, congregation or group who pays heed to them. Once established in their lives, these demons dominate them through these damnable heresies. Such people get deeply deceived and also go on to deceive others (1 Tim. 3:13). Ultimately and historically, the result of such bewitchment is unimaginable harm. Once again, we must test all spirits in order to keep ourselves from doctrines of demons. When such false doctrines are received, they are received together with the demons behind them.

4. Exposure to New Age culture

The new age culture is a significant influence in contemporary society. As a movement, the new age is arguably the fastest growing religious network in today's world. It is a loosely structured movement of noted individuals and religious organizations zealous to promote a "worldwide view and vision of the new age of enlightenment and harmony," otherwise knows as "the age of Aquarius."[1]

In advancing this age of "enlightenment," new age proponents have infiltrated every sector of secular human endeavor, including as education, health, entertainment/media, finance and other sectors of the global economy. In bringing about this worldview of enlightenment and harmony, they seek a revivalism and modernization of ancient Oriental, Buddhist, Hindu, and Egyptian mystical and occultist practices. In essence, these are aspects of occultism specially made to attract the modern person in a non-religious setting.

New Age practices include yoga, transcendental meditation, acupuncture, acupressure, certain forms of massage and touch therapy, and certain elements of exercise, fitness, and health practices. Magic, hypnotism, horror movies, certain forms of secular TV entertainment or Internet-based ungodly entertainment, the sex industry, children's toys such as Pikachu and Pokémon, various forms of secular music, especially heavy metal, rap, disco, and forms of reggae, and also certain aspects of martial arts including Kung Fu, karate, and judo exercises are based on aspects of new age culture.

Concerning this present age, the apostle had this to say, "But the evil men and seducers shall wax worse and worse deceiving and being deceived" (2 Tim. 3:13). The words *seducers* or *impostors* in some modern versions literally mean "enchanters." These enchanters use chants to deceive people. In very typical form, these chants are "incantations." Interestingly, most of today's music, especially rock and rap, use demonic chants or incantations in their lyrics to seduce and alter people's minds, thus exposing them to demons. I once encountered a young boy aged approximately thirteen who was tormented by suicidal thoughts. When interrogated during counseling, he confessed to playing heavy metal rock music shortly before he came under this torment, and he pointed out that the lyrics were filled with words of "death." The boy's mother validated these claims. However, to the glory of God, when I challenged these demons in the mighty name of the Lord Jesus Christ, they came out of him and he was delivered. My explanation is that he was exposed to the demons of death and suicide through the heavy metal chants. This is applicable to other forms of exposure to the new age practices. All new age practices listed earlier expose their practitioners to demonic invasion, and subsequently to oppression, control, and bondage.

5. Drug addiction

Addiction to illicit drugs and other forms of substance abuse opens the abuser to demonic influences. Most of these substances are not only habit forming, but also mind altering. In other words, when the user is first hooked up with these substances, he or she is brought under the first level of demonic bondage. This initial bondage is basically the victim's inability to do without the substance. At this point, demons subject the person to intense cravings for the substance in question. Having brought the individual under such degree of compulsive dependence on the substance, the stage is then set for the second level of demonic bondage and domination: the systematic alteration of the victim's mind and thought process. When the mind is altered in this way, it is given over to all forms of evil and negative behavioral, socio-economic, and relationship patterns that defy civility and godliness.

Moreover, the eroded protection over such minds leads to an invasion by all forms of related demons such as those of immorality, violence, suicide, rejection, rebellion, poverty, and hopelessness. This is a classic example of a person breaking the defensive wall and letting the serpent in to bite him or her (Eccl. 10:8). The contemporary drug culture targeted against young people is a demonically fashioned instrument to manipulate, dominate, and destroy a whole generation. This contemporary drug culture is, in fact, a form of sorcery, which is in itself witchcraft and occultism. In Revelation 9:20, John the Apostle described the fate of a section of humanity who came under divine judgment for various forms of evil practices, all of which are already prevalent in our present age. These practices, including worship of demons and idols, occultism, and materialism, had a serious hold on the people to the extent that they could not repent, "And they did not repent of their murders... sorceries...immorality...theft" (Rev. 9:21).

Notice the prevalence and interrelatedness of these evil acts in our modern society. However, a closer look at the word *sorceries* is very illuminating. In the Greek, the word is *pharmakeia*, meaning pharmacy or medication. In a literal or figurative sense by extension, sorceries can be rendered as magic, sorcery, or witchcraft.

The same word was also used in Revelation 18:23 when John comments on the fall of Babylon as a result of God's judgment. The reason for the city's judgment was her wickedness in deceiving the world with "sorceries." With this understanding, I personally believe that drug addiction is not merely a social problem but a form of sorcery. By this form of sorcery, which is different from its twin, enchantments, demons cast spells on people's minds and dominate or control them.

These demons get in when people step into the world of drugs including prescription medications or other addictive substances such as alcohol, mostly for initial reasons of peer pressure, curiosity, or frustration. Once they gain access to the minds of such curious people, these demons proceed to dominate, control, and alter their minds.

6. Tattoos and body marks

Tattoos and other forms of marking the body are also forms of occultism, which coexist with those already described. Clearly, most of the pictures, words, and graffiti images inscribed on body parts as tattoos cannot be from the true Christ, but are a prelude to the coming "mark of the beast" (Rev. 14:9–11; 16:2). These marks usually portray pornography, obscenity, violence, and other evil works or images. Among tribal peoples around the world, most body marks entail a lancet incision on the skin, squeezing out of the blood, and implantation of some demonically empowered substance into the body. The blood squeezed out is offered to demons for an initiation or covenant. Also, tattoo images invite the related spirits into the bearer's life. For instance, a pornographic tattoo image invites the spirits of immorality into the life of the bearer.

Also, such a bearer becomes a living expression of the spirit of immorality. He or she is bound by and serves the spirit of immorality (Rom. 6:13, 19). Non-tattoo body marks are mostly procured by lancet and leave permanent scars afterwards. They are usually made in the course of procuring evil covenants with demons, especially among animists and other tribal people among African and Asian cultures. This motivation is becoming more and more prevalent on the Euro-American scene. These marks are the exit portals of the blood of such idol worshipers and entry portals of the relevant demonic ingredients.

In essence, these marks represent and remind everybody involved in such rituals of the "laying down" or the submission of the worshiper's life to the idol and its respective demons. On the basis of such submission, the worshiper becomes enslaved, dominated, and controlled by those demons with the manifestation of all forms of evil inheritance. This evil power or domination can only be terminated and broken when and if the victim repents, accepts Jesus Christ as Lord and Savior, and comes under the most efficacious blood of Jesus Christ offered though the eternal Spirit (Rom. 6:13; 4:22–25; 5:9–10).

Recently I read about an unfortunate incident in a renowned city newspaper about a young man who went to a tattoo salon and requested for a certain tattoo image known as Last Rites. On the completion of this artwork, he fell upon a glass case and bled to death. I believe this was a spirit of death invited and released by the Last Rites tattoo. This is a form of covenant with death.

7. Names

One of the most practical and effective ways through which demons gain access into and dominate and manipulate peoples' destinies is through the kind of names people bear. You may ask, "What's in a name?" But in the Bible, and among many cultures around the world names have meaning and strongly determine and influence the character, nature and destiny of the one bearing the name (1 Sam. 25:23–25). A name can have either negative or positive connotations. If a name has a negative or evil connotation, it attracts relevant evil forces or spirits behind it, which work out the evil character and destiny that name represents. In fact, a name is a description or actualization of a potential destiny. To take a name with a negative and evil meaning is to make a pact with the spirits or forces behind such names. The pact invites such spirits into the life of the bearer, and in this way the bearer gets enslaved and acts out the nature, character, and destiny of those spirits. Moreover, each time the name is called out or used, such confessions or professions release evil forces associated with such names to work out negative and evil destiny and to glorify evil.

On the other hand, a change of name can bring about a change in nature, character, and destiny. In fact, God had to change the names of some: of His servants from the negative to the positive. Abram, Sarai, Jacob, and Saul of Tarsus are such examples. God is glorified in their new names: Abraham, Sarah, Jacob, and Paul, respectively, as evidenced by their experience of deliverance and transformation in their lives following the name change.

8. Possession of fetish or cursed objects

This is another common access route used by demons into human lives. A fetish is usually an inanimate object associated with some mystical power. The Bible calls such objects "accursed objects" or "things under the ban" because they are devoted to idols. Due to their dedication to idols, these objects are cursed, doomed and set apart for destruction. God's people are strictly forbidden from having any form of contact with them (Josh. 6:18). Israel's experience at Ai reveals God's attitude toward such objects, "But the children of Israel committed a trespass in the accursed thing: for Achan...took of the accursed thing; and the anger of the Lord was kindled against the children of Israel" (Josh. 7:1).

Achan's action was indeed a direct trespass to God's Word. In Joshua 6:18, God had warned against taking the accursed thing and the consequences of disobedience, "And ye, in any wise keep yourselves from the accursed thing, lest ye make yourselves accursed when ye take of the accursed thing and make the camp of Israel a curse and trouble it." Achan's trespass brought defeat upon Israel. From this experience, the following lessons are significant:

- God's people must keep themselves from accursed objects
- Contact with accursed objects defiles the individual and brings him or her under a curse
- Such a defilement and curse also brings consequences upon those in the immediate environment or in fellowship.

A deliberate acquisition or contact with accursed objects initiates a pact: or covenant between the individual and evil spirits behind such objects. Such evil covenants negate God's claim over the person, and on the basis of such rebellion God withdraws His divine presence, covenant, and protection.

> Therefore, the children of Israel could not stand before their enemies, because they were accursed— neither will I (God) be with you any more, except ye destroy the accursed from among you.
> —Joshua 7:12

Some of the categories of accursed things commonly in use today include:

- Inherited objects: ancestral and traditional religious objects, certain titles and dedicated trees, and monuments or landmarks inherited through rites of lineage to traditional religious figures or persons and cultures

- Artwork: certain form of artwork especially those with horrifying or other negative images such as snakes, dragons, other beasts and zodiac signs (These may also include certain forms of posters, photographs and charts.)

- Real estate: personal and public houses, land, and other forms of real estate dedicated to idols and ritual practices (Some of these properties were dedicated right from the stage of architectural designing and foundation. Sometimes, personal properties used for such religious purposes such as furniture and clothing may also be accursed.)

Sincere people sometimes inadvertently come in contact with accursed objects. If such people turn to the Lord Jesus for direction, He will open their eyes by the Holy Spirit. I personally suggest that everyone reading this book examine his or her house. Ask the Holy Spirit to put His finger on any accursed object in your life, house, car, or any other belongings. A house cleaning may be necessary. A careful look into your jewelry box may surprise you. You may have to get rid of those things that bear ungodly images. Some of the images, carvings, or posters or pictures in your home may have to go. If you must buy used articles, you need the guidance of the Holy Spirit before proceeding. Houses and other forms of real estate may have to be cleansed by prayer and rededicated to the Lord Jesus Christ (2 Cor. 6:14–18). God's prescription for dealing with graven images is a bonfire!

> The graven images of their gods shall ye burn with fire: thou shall not desire the silver or gold that is in them, nor take it unto thee lest thou be snared therein: for it is an abomination to the Lord thy God. Neither shall thou bring an abomination in thy house, lest thou be a cursed thing like it; but thou shall utterly detest it, and thou shall utterly abhor it; for it is a cursed thing.
>
> —Deuteronomy 7:25–26

> And many that believed, came and confessed and shewed their deeds. Many of them also which used curious arts brought their books together, and burned them before all men: and they counted the price of them, and found them fifty thousand pieces of silver.
>
> —Acts 19:18–19

6

BROKEN BORDERS: PART II

W E WILL CONTINUE with our discussion of Broken Borders, begun in chapter 5.

9. Evil covenants

One of the most basic avenues through which demons gain access into a human life is the cutting of covenants between a person and an idol. This is the process of initiating people into idolatrous and occult religious practices. Such covenants are an expression of commitment and submission between the person and the idol or false deity. All such covenants are unholy and evil before the true God (Jehovah). Furthermore, these evil covenants defy God's sacred covenants revealed in the Bible, which culminated in the New Covenant. The severity of God's attitude toward these unholy covenants is also revealed in the Bible, "Take heed to thyself, lest thou make a covenant with the inhabitants of the land whither thou goest, lest it be a snare in the midst of thee. But ye shall destroy their altars, break their images and cut down their grooves. For thou shall worship no other god: for the Lord whose name is Jealous is a jealous God" (Exod. 34:12–14).

Characteristically, worshipers of false gods systematically and surreptitiously seek to entice worshippers of the true God into idolatry and occultism. One of the ways they do this is through a covenant relationship not of God, which includes all forms of spiritual relationship between a person or persons and an idol. Such a relationship is prone to lead to two kinds of abomination among God's people:

First, a tolerance for accursed objects of idolatry and the occult.

Second, direct involvement in the worship of idols, which is a serious apostasy since God Himself has already made sacred covenants with His chosen people.

A covenant with idols or demons is a pact with death (sheol, or the grave) and it is a deception (Isa. 28:15–18). Also by its very nature, a covenant with a false deity brings someone into an oneness of flesh, soul, and spirit with such deity (1 Cor. 6:14–20; 2 Cor. 6:14–18). Beyond this personal concord and fellowship with demons through evil covenants, such persons also come under divine judgment and expose their posterity to God's curse and demonic domination. Millions of people are suffering today because of past evil covenants their ancestors made with false deities. Such covenants and their evil consequences are binding on families, kindred, or groups of people up till the fourth generation (Exod. 20:1–5). It is only the precious blood of Jesus Christ that can annul such covenants and free their victims from demonic harassment and other forms of evil inheritance. Jesus Christ as God's sacrificial Lamb offered His blood (Himself) to God on our behalf, in order to institute the only true and permanent covenant acceptable to God, known as the New Covenant or New Testament. Before He went to the cross, He said, "Drink from it, all of you, for this is my blood of the covenant, which is poured out for many for the forgiveness of sins" (Matt. 26:27–28).

After His death the writer of Hebrews had this to say concerning this covenant, "For by one offering (sacrifice) He has perfected for all time those who are sanctified" (Heb. 10:14).

The Lord Jesus Christ ministers continually today before God almighty as the High Priest of God who leads everyone who comes to Him into His New Covenant. This New Covenant, which is revealed in a shadow first in the Old Testament of the Holy Bible, and then fulfilled in the New Testament, is a better covenant because it is based on better promises and is mediated by the only High Priest who has access to God the Father (Heb. 1:3; 3:1; 4:14–16; 5:5; 8:1–3; 9:11–14). The only religious experience based on this New Covenant is biblical Christianity (Heb. 8:4–6; 12:2).

Some of the false religious practices through which people are brought into evil covenants include:

- solemn verbal oath taking, especially with non-Christians or servants of Satan and those procured for membership in secret societies

- all religious rituals and ceremonies that have no New Testament biblical basis or support

- repeated participation in non-Christian, non-biblical forms of religious worship and/or secret societies

- possession of and sustained contact with fetishes and accursed objects

- participation in all forms of occult practices such as horoscopy, palm reading, consulting with psychics and diviners, holding séances, using mediums, and necromancy

- all forms of blood oaths (evil blood covenants including those used by lovers to enter into marriage and friendship relationships or soul ties)

- demonic baptism (the practice of bathing or
  immersing people into water by false prophets
  and idol worshippers in the name of idols). This
  is a counterfeit of Christian water baptism by
  immersion.

- dream covenants, regular patterns of the
  following activities in dreams: eating, sexual
  intercourse, visitation by "spirit spouses,"
  pregnancy/miscarriage cycles in the dream,
  encounters with snakes, dogs, masquerades; also
  running, flying and swimming, etc.

- offerings or gifts in cash or other material objects
  to any deity other than the Lord Jesus Christ,
  God's appointed High Priest

- certain so-called entertainment treats such as
  hypnosis and all forms of Halloween activities, including mock burial rituals (the practice
  of putting living persons in a casket or in a
  grave, which is also counterfeit of Christianity's
  doctrine of burial with Christ through water
  baptism)

10. Wrong relationship

A wrong relationship for our present purpose will simply
refer to an inappropriate relationship between any two people
or group of people. By inappropriate I mean that the Bible
strictly forbids such a relationship. These relationships not only
result in a dishonoring of God's name, but also ultimately lead
to self-destruction. Some of the more common forms of wrong
relationship include:

- sexual: adultery, fornication, homosexuality, bestiality, and incest
- mixed marriages between Christian believers and non-Christians (not including cases where two people got married as non-believers and one later repents and believes in the Lord Jesus)
- casual, non-marital commitments leading to compromise, sin, and evil
- any deliberate relationship of commitment with a known practitioner of occult and other forms of idolatry

There are many other forms of such "unequal yokes." Some were rampant in the church in Corinth when Paul wrote, "What agreement has the temple of God with idols? For ye are the temple of the living God. Just as God said I will dwell in them and work among them; and I will be their God and they shall be my people" (2 Cor. 6:16–17).

Here, we understand that Christian believers are God's temple and carry God's presence, the Holy Spirit, within them. In the fourteenth verse, Paul refers to these forms of relationship as a binding together, suggesting a spiritual union or yoke between a believer and an unbeliever. In verses 15 and 16, Paul describes this relationship as partnership, fellowship (communion), concord or accord (harmony), and agreement. In other words, when we as believers enter into wrong relationship, we rob Christ of our body, which in fact belongs to Him. Literally, we expel Him from His temple and end up turning what belongs to Jesus Christ into a sacrilege. Notice that the entities Paul compares are basically spiritual entities, namely righteousness versus unrighteousness or lawlessness, light versus darkness, Christ versus Baal, God versus idols.

In Paul's first epistle to this same church in Corinth, he rebukes sexual immorality while also dwelling on this same theme, "Do you not know that your bodies are members of Christ? Shall I then take away the members of Christ and make them members of a harlot? May it never be! Or do you not know that the one who joins himself to a harlot is one body with her? For He says, 'The two will become one flesh: but the one who joins himself to the Lord is one spirit with Him'" (1 Cor. 6:16–17).

The one who joins with a harlot—in a wrong relationship—is of one body with the harlot. The operative law in this case is "two shall become one," bound together and ruled by the same spirit. On the other hand, when we yield our bodies to the Lord through pure and right relationship, we are united with the Lord by the one and only Holy Spirit. There is always a spirit behind every relationship; we may open ourselves up to unclean spirits through the company we keep.

11. Laying on of hands

This is an enduring spiritual exercise, which can have a powerful impact on the person ministering it or receiving it. Millions of people today owe a lot to this act. Historically, from the patriarchal age till now, it remains a common channel of impartation of spiritual gifts, ministry gifts, healing and other forms of blessing among God's people (1 Tim. 1:4; 4:14; 5:22). It is a foundational New Testament doctrine (Heb. 6:1–2).

However, the laying on of hands can be abused both in and outside the church. Moreover, Satan's servants use it overtly and covertly to release evil spirits upon people, thus bringing them under a curse, sickness, calamity, bondage, and even death.

Modern new age techniques for healing and other forms of spirituality include "touch," which supposedly releases some form of spiritual "energy." Sometimes this form of touch avoids actual physical contact with the body of the recipient. In any case we must be a lot more discerning in order to separate good from evil. At all times, when hands are about to be laid, it is the personal responsibility of the potential recipient in such a service to seek God's mind with regard to the character, life-style, and religious background of the person or minister doing it. The way and manner in which the hands are being laid is also instructive.

Extra-biblical forms of laying on of hands, especially in eastern traditional religions or new age settings, are purported to release some form of spiritual energy and maintain holistic balance. Even though these have received great endorsement from both health experts and religious leaders, as long as they are a form of spirituality that does not subscribe to the sole lord-ship of Jesus Christ and are not inspired by the Holy Spirit, they are purely, simply demonic. I believe that anyone who submits himself or herself to such therapy is exposed to demons. The Spirit of the true God—the Holy Spirit—is a Person and not an energy. Any use of new age terminology such as spiritual energy is alien to the person and work of the Holy Spirit. The spirit at work in such cases must be demons.

12. Curses

A curse is an imposition of evil or a negative wish or destiny upon a person or group of people, including entire families, communities, nations, or races, as well as human institutions and organizations. Even animals and trees may come under curses. Inorganic entities or objects may also be cursed; typical examples are houses and plots of land.

Usually, curses are imposed through proclamations, written statements, or by divinations, incantations, or spells. Ulti-mately, the intention is to bring affliction or harm on the target or targets. When such invocations are made, unclean spirits are actually released to accomplish the intended affliction, harm, or evil in the life and affairs of the victim. The victim, having been thus brought under demonic bondage, experiences the activity of such demonic forces at work in their lives. For the purpose of this book, I will give a few examples of curses commonly at work in people:

a. Generational curses: curses inherited from ancestors, parents, grandparents, uncles, aunts, and other relations (Exod. 20:2–5)

b. Self-invoked curses: curses that individuals bring upon themselves. These are usually affected through negative language focusing on personal failures, low self-esteem, inadequacy, sickness, and hopelessness. Other modalities of invocation include oaths and acceptance of jinxes (Gen. 27:1–13; Num. 14:26–30; Matt. 12:36–37). When our language about ourselves is in negatives, demons are released against us to execute such expressions. On the other hand, when our confession about ourselves lines up with God's promises or purposes concerning us, the Lord Jesus Christ, who is the Apostle and High Priest of our confession or profession, releases the Holy Spirit to accomplish God's will and plan in us and for us.

c. "Friendly Fire": I personally use this phrase for those curses that are unintentionally made by one upon one's family members, friends, and other close relations due to ignorance of the truth of a situation or circumstances. One of the most common scenarios is the idea of a person swearing with a curse in defense of someone he or she loves. A classic example is the case of Jacob unintentionally cursing Rachel, his wife, while defending her against her father's accusations regarding a missing household idol (Gen. 31:22–32; 35:16–19). This incident is believed by many to be contributory to Rachel's untimely death during childbirth. She named the child Benomi, son of my sorrow (although his father renamed him Benjamin, the son of my right hand).

d. Authority figure curses: these are curses imposed by someone in position of authority on the people under their leadership. Examples of such figures are parents, teachers, pastors and other religious leaders, political leaders and kings. Also, the subjects of a king or political leader may also curse the leader (Prov. 11:26). The following are some of the major examples of authority figure curses in the Bible:

- First, the patriarch Isaac's words to Esau (Gen. 27:37–40);

- Second, Joshua's words to any prospective re-builders of the city of Jericho (Josh. 6:26–27; 1 Kings 16:34);

- Third, the word of the religious leaders in rejecting Jesus Christ the innocent before Pilate and accepting Barabbas, a criminal. When they rejected Jesus, they rejected all His goodness, holiness, innocence, blessings, and peace. In Barabbas, they accepted rebellion, unrighteousness, curses, and violence. With all their spiritual authority, they invoked a curse not only upon themselves, but also upon their upcoming generations when Pilate dissociated himself from the case and from an impending injustice, "And when Pilate saw that he was accomplishing nothing, but rather a riot was starting, he took water and washed his hands in front of the multitude, saying, 'I am innocent of this man's blood, see to that yourselves.' And all the people answered and said, 'His blood be on us and our children!'" (Matt. 27:24–25).Many people today believe that the negative destinies of the descendents of these religious leaders are a result of these self-imposed curses, which also qualify as authority figure curses since they included their posterity under the curse.

- Fourth, authority figures such as parents and teachers who yell out curse words or even negatives such as you will never make it or you are no good. These words release relevant evil forces that shape the destiny of their subjects in the direction of failure. Godly authority figures must desist from cursing their subjects. God has called us to bless. Bear in mind that curses release demons in the lives of their targets.

13. Spells

Spells are evil magic formulas or satanic curses used to bind, oppose, or afflict people. This is a form of witchcraft employed to dominate, manipulate, and ultimately cause harm. Like other forms of curses, spells may variously be released via enchantment, entrancement, divination, and incantation. Just as the Lord Jesus Christ has commissioned His servants to go into the world blessing, healing, and delivering people from demons and praying for the release of the Holy Spirit, so has Satan commissioned his own human servants to do the opposite.

The ministry of Balak and Balaam against God and Israel is a classic example of the activity of Satan's human servants against God and humanity, particularly the church. Balaam's primary devices were divination and enchantment (Num. 23:23). These devices are still in use today in order to release demons and other evil forces. I believe that if Balaam's mission and action were insignificant, God would not have bothered to intervene on behalf of Israel. Typically, Satan's human servants in this present day seek to oppose the movement of God and God's people. In this way, they try to keep God's people from their inheritance and seek to afflict them with mishap, calamity, disunity, failure, and affliction.

Today, Satan's human servants—witches, wizards, Babalawos, obiaman, shaman, voodoo and Santeria priests and worshipers, worshipers of other idols, psychics, diviners, and all other forms of occult practitioners—seek to dominate and manipulate society, and oppose the church through their demonic spells (Num. 22:23).

Other forms of curses may result from:

- anti-Semitic attitudes (Gen. 12:2–3; Num. 24:9)
- legalism/carnality (Jer. 17:5–6)

- apostasy (Jer. 17:5)
- cheating God in tithes and offerings (Hag. 1:4–6; Mal. 3:8–9); withholding offerings and tithes from God invariably releases the demon spirit known as the devourer, which operates through insufficiency, lack, and wasting.

But thanks be to God who always gives us victory through the cross of Calvary. He gave us the blood of Jesus Christ under the authority of which we constantly overcome Satan and all his forces. God's destiny for believers in Christ Jesus is blessing. This blessing becomes ours in Christ and in experience when we renounce and revoke curses, break their power over us, and then receive God's blessings. This freedom is only obtainable by faith in Jesus Christ and submission to the Holy Spirit. This faith in Christ Jesus receives with humility the fact that, "Christ redeemed us from the curse of the law, having become a curse for us, for it is written, cursed is everyone who hangs on a tree" (Gal. 3:13).

The result of this incredible divine transaction is most awesome. Concerning this, Paul explains, "In order that in Christ Jesus, the blessing of Abraham might come on the Gentiles, so that we might receive the promise of the Spirit through faith" (Gal. 3:14).

14. Overindulgence in natural appetites

Most natural appetites are inherently good and usually draw us to pure values and gratification. However, overindulgence even in the things that are naturally good suggests the activity of spirits, "All things are lawful unto me, but all things are not expedient. All things are lawful for me but I will not be brought under the power of any" (1 Cor. 6:12). In this verse of Scripture, the apostle Paul expresses a legitimate freedom to gratify every good, natural appetite; but he also observes that such a freedom is not always profitable. Furthermore, he identifies another inherently dangerous element or experience the freedom may lead to, and that is being brought "under the power" of these appetites. In other words, otherwise positive, natural appetites can have a dominating power or influence over the human will.

The dominating power or influence is a spirit; hence it can overwhelm a person, resulting in a cycle of sin. In this way, such natural, legitimate appetites become weights and encumber us. While still non-sinful in themselves, weights constitute burdens, or yokes, which ultimately get us to sin against God, forget Him, or distract us from our heavenly focus and value. These weights undermine our Christian race. The Hebrew believers in Jesus were enjoined as follows, "Let us lay aside every weight and the sin which doth so easily beset us, and let us run with patience the race that is set before us" (Heb. 12:1).

A few examples of natural and positive appetites in which we may overindulge include eating, drinking, sleeping, marriage, career, investments, sports, and other forms of recreation. Most of these are the marks of the days of Noah—the spirit and age of materialism. In Galatians 5:23, the opposite attitude to over-indulgence—temperance, or self-control—is the character and mark of the Spirit of Jesus Christ, the sovereign Holy Spirit. When we overstep the bounds of common sense, self-control, or temperance, we are exposed to the "spirit of overindulgence," a demon that works by compulsion and addiction. In Paul's language, to be under compulsion or addiction is to be brought under the power of a demonic spirit.

15. Sinful habits

Another practical doorway for demons is the deliberate and repeated indulgence in sinful habits and attitudes. It is true that Satan is the one who primarily tempts us to commit sin against

God. However, God has given us the ability to resist Satan and overcome temptation. This power is found in Jesus through the Holy Spirit. The option that faces every individual in temptation is either to yield to God or to Satan. Yielding is an exercise of the will. When the will is so exercised, it results in a decision.

Whenever we make a decision and yield to a spirit, person or value, the very spirit behind such a person or value binds us, "Do you not know that when you present (yield) yourselves to someone as slave for obedience, you are slaves to the one whom you obey, either of sin resulting in death or of obedience resulting in righteousness?" (Rom. 6:16).

The negative force in us that craves evil and unrighteousness is the flesh. The flesh is the fallen, sinful nature in every person. It is also known as the "old man." This degenerate, corrupt nature has a very high affinity for demons. The evil influence of the flesh in the human life can be brought under subjection by:

- knowing that Jesus Christ crucified the flesh on the cross and thus rendered sin powerless (Rom. 6:6);

- reckoning regularly with the above historical fact in our personal lives (Rom. 6:11);

- and, on the basis of the first two facts, appropriating God's grace by the Holy Spirit and exercising a continual personal victory over the flesh and sin through general spiritual discipline. Some specific steps include obedience to the word, prayer, and fasting (1 Cor. 9:27; Gal. 5:24).

A personal failure to tame the flesh puts the individual at the mercy of the flesh, so he or she becomes a slave of the flesh who indulges in sinful habits such as immorality, strife, anger, jealousy, gossip, dissension, disputes, substance abuse, and occult practices (Gal. 5:17–23). Someone may be drawn to any of these experiences through sheer curiosity and lack of discipline. Initially, these activities may be the result of a deliberate conscious decision of the will; but later, as willpower dissipates, the individual progressively loses the power to say no. In this way, there is degeneration from sensuality to demonic bondage. This is unfortunately characterized by an entrenched cycle of bondage and frustration:

> For just as you presented (yielded) your members as slaves to impurity and to lawlessness (iniquity) resulting in further lawlessness.
>
> —ROMANS 6:19

At this stage, the victim often finds himself or herself in a state of sinning, confessing, and committing the same sin again. Usually, he or she is still bound even after repeated confession of sins, fasting, and counseling. Deliverance from demons may be considered at this point, and help sought through a valid deliverance ministry involving follow-up counseling sessions.

I also need to point out that after the initial experience of salvation, the Christian believer is still challenged by a moment-to-moment decision as to whom to obey. As believers continue to yield to the Lord Jesus Christ, the Holy Spirit who indwells us continues to assert His power over every area of our lives. In this way we continue to experience growth in grace. However, when we yield to the flesh any area or part of our lives, we are open to demonic invasions. Hence it is possible for demons to operate in any area of the believer's life not yielded to the Lord.

16. Emotional crisis

A great deal of a person's outlook in life results from various kinds of crisis experience. Such exposures or experiences constitute major doorways for demons into the human spirit unless they are handled in a godly way. Common examples of such experiences are pre-natal and post-natal life experiences, discussed below.

Pre-natal emotional experience

In God's perspective, life begins even before conception in the womb (Jer. 2:5). The fetus in the womb is a person known of God, set apart and called for a purpose. God's provision for that life includes a network of strong anatomical and physiological links to the mother's biological resources for its physical well-being. Maternal spiritual and emotional resources are also an essential source of supply and support for spiritual and emotional needs and well-being of the life in the womb during pregnancy. Any form of corruption, withdrawal, or outright termination of such spiritual and emotional support also adversely affects the outlook or destiny of this unborn child. Therefore, exposing the unborn child to any of the following negative and evil attitudes and environment will open him or her up to evil spiritual influences and bring the child under demonic manipulation or bondage later in life:

- idolatry and occultism, such as evil covenants; negative names; dedication of the unborn child to idols and ritual practices; use of occult concoctions and certain herbal medicinal substances in the course of the parents' quest for conception through witch doctors

- parental exposure to sinful acts or habits during pregnancy, such as use of pornography, adultery, and other forms of immorality

- pre-natal exposure to horror experiences during pregnancy, such as horror movies, masquerades, evil festivals, domestic violence, accident and disaster scenes

- unkind and harsh attitudes to the unborn child by either or both parents and other relations, including negative words toward the unborn child or even the mother, and parental disappointment concerning the sex of the baby, leading to contemplated or attempted termination of pregnancy.

Most of the above attitudes are common parental or family reactions in cases of "unwanted pregnancy." Such pregnancies are said to be unwanted because of certain adverse circumstances surrounding them: unexpected pregnancy, single parenthood, or pregnancies resulting from rape. Marital separation and domestic violence or tension are also common reasons for such unfavorable attitudes toward the unborn child. Demons of rejection, low self-esteem, bitterness, shame, rebellion, witchcraft, bisexuality, and homosexuality are common opportunists in such situations.

Post-natal emotional experience

These are emotional crisis experiences that confront an individual from birth through childhood to adulthood. The most common among these experiences are:

- Disappointment: scars of disappointments, when sustained, may break the protective hedge and permit exposure to spirits of shame, low self-esteem, inferiority, hopelessness, discouragement, unworthiness, bitterness, doubt, unbelief, mistrust, cynicism, criticism, rejection, depression, and suicide. The most common causes of disappointment include parental abandonment of children, spousal abandonment, divorce, separation, broken engagement vows, and personal failures of self, significant others, mentors, and authority figures.

- Stress: drains spiritual and emotional vitality and opens the door to spirits of heaviness (depression), uncertainty, hopelessness, gloom, restlessness, tension, sleeplessness, and fear. Spirits of infirmity may be bred in situations of stress and may manifest in chronic chest pain, back pain, hypertension, migraine, peptic ulcers, bronchial asthma, chronic fatigue, muscle pains, or dysmenorrhea.

- Emotional shock: generally, some forms of acute negative emotional experiences such as incest, rape, molestation, abortion, and spousal infidelity readily bring in spirits of guilt, lust, homosexuality, condemnation, shame, self-pity, rejection, hate, resentment, rebellion, low self-esteem, unforgiveness, and retaliation.

- Unpleasant appointments: appointments with certain emotionally unpleasant or dreadful events often lead to intense fear that can paralyze the spiritual and emotional defenses of the individual. When such fears are sustained over

time, faith is overthrown and the spirit: of fear
dominates.

- The spirit of fear always recruits its associates:
  spirits of death, accidents, and failure, disaster,
  mishap, and calamity. Common unpleasant
  emotional events and experiences include
  airplane flights, academic and professional evaluation tests, stage performances, contests, dental
  or surgical procedures, and anesthesia. Typically,
  extreme fear before anesthesia, surgery, or minor
  medical and dental procedures may open the
  patient up to a spirit of death or mishaps leading
  to death and complications. In most cases,
  such complications or mishaps are scientifically
  unexplainable.

- A normally simple, uneventful, and safe proce-
  dure or venture gradually or suddenly becomes
  stormy, and everything goes wrong; even the
  experts are baffled and helpless in such cases.
  The experience of Job in Job 3:5, "For what I fear
  comes upon me, and what I dread befalls me,"
  is a lesson to all who regularly entertain and
  yield to fear. Concerning our overall emotional
  balance, God's provision is expressed in Paul's
  letter to Timothy, "For God has not given us a
  spirit of fear (timidity), but of power and love
  and discipline (sound mind)" (2 Tim. 1:7).

Notice that fear is a spirit, not a mere psychological concept.
Fear is not: to be treated as an intangible, impersonal mist,
but as a person. It should be resisted, rebuked, and cast out.
Furthermore, where fear operates, the power of the individual

becomes paralyzed; the capacity for faith and to love is drained, and judgment becomes irrational. In other words, the entire emotional setup is destabilized. These are results of fear when admitted into our lives. One of God's major weapons against fear is obedience to the Holy Spirit: the true Spirit.

> Perfect love (obedience) casts out fear.
>
> —1 JOHN 4:18

Furthermore, our inheritance as descendents of Abraham and Sarah includes our refusal to be frightened by any fear: "Thus Sarah obeyed Abraham, calling him Lord, and you have become her children if you do what is right without being frightened by any fear" (1 Pet. 3:6). The only fear the believer is called to observe is the reverence of the true God. As humans we do experience moments of fear, but we should not continue to entertain it; otherwise it will grow to such extreme states as described above through the demon of fear.

17. Unforgiveness

Unforgiveness is a potent doorway to spirits of bitterness, hate, murder, violence, criticism, stress, depression, torment, retaliation, pain, and various sorts of emotional and physical infirmity. Unforgiveness shuts the one who indulges in it out of the grace, mercy, and forgiveness of God. Essentially, it hinders prayer. In fact, if one is shut out of God's grace, mercy, and forgiveness, one lacks peace and overall well-being. Often, it is not humanly possible to forgive, and this is where all of us need God's grace and help to forgive those who hurt and offend us. Indeed, we need God's love and grace shed in our hearts to forgive others. However, since God has shed His love in our hearts, He demands that we make the personal decision to forgive. In this sense, forgiveness is a decision to use God's grace for the benefit of others and ours.

> And so, as those who have been chosen of God, holy and beloved, put on a heart of compassion, kindness, humility, gentleness and patience; bearing with one another, and forgiving each other, whoever has a complaint against anyone; just as the Lord forgave you, so also should you.
>
> —COLOSSIANS 3:12–13

When we fail to forgive, we will rob ourselves of the blessing of answered prayers and will open ourselves up to tormentors. Demons are tormentors in every respect and they will always exploit our failure to forgive to hurt us (Matt. 18:34–35; Mark 11:25–26).

7

DEMONIC BONDAGE

T HE MANIFESTATION OF Satan's power and dominion over humanity is also referred to as the kingdom (or power) of darkness. Humanity for its part and by itself was helpless in the sense that it could neither change its degenerate state nor resist the overwhelming presence power and operation of evil that subsequently enveloped it. Humanity and all of creation henceforth came under a curse principle. I believe this principle was what Paul described as the "law of sin and of death" (Rom. 8:2). In my understanding, this is the state of bondage. It is on the basis of this law and state that Satan set up a kingdom to administer this dispensation of darkness, hopelessness, and captivity of the human race. This evil kingdom reigned through sin, sickness, various forms of demonic oppressions, and death until the manifestation, death, and resurrection of Christ Jesus the savior. Concerning this Paul writes, "For if by the transgression of the one (Adam), death reigned through the one, much more those who receive the abundance of grace and of the gift of righteousness will reign in life through the one Jesus Christ" (Rom. 5:17).

Before the manifestation of Jesus and His finished work on the cross, Satan and his cohorts exercised dominion over humanity through death, which is representative of sin, sickness, and other forms of bondage. However, after the death,

101

resurrection, and ascension of Jesus, any member of the human race who receives His sacrifice as the only means of salvation is not only saved from sin but also has received abundance of grace and the gift of righteousness. The believer also partakes of the royalty of Christ with which he or she now reigns over Satan, fallen angels, demons, and other forces of darkness. Therefore, any person or thing not yet yielded to the Lord Jesus is still subject to Satan's bondage and dominion. In the case of persons or lives that have been yielded to Christ, Satan's power and dominion have been broken and terminated. Furthermore, through a continued exercise of faith in Christ Jesus, this freedom becomes a continuing and ever-expanding personal experience. This life of freedom in Christ is the blessing principle, which Paul likewise described as the "law of the Spirit of life in Christ Jesus" (Rom. 8:2). This blessing or life principle was obtained at the resurrection of Christ and fully released at Pentecost and has remained in force under the administration of the sovereign Holy Spirit.

Unfortunately, with the veil of spiritual ignorance, Satan is now actively at work hindering souls from seeing the light of the gospel of Jesus and the blessing and freedom it brings (2 Cor. 4:3–4). Subsequently, millions of people remain in bondage.

Demons constitute a major force through which this bondage is perpetuated. For this reason, by the grace of God, I will devote the rest of this chapter to the topic of demonic bondage.

DAIMONIZOMAI

Demonic bondage means to be under the power, authority, or influence of demons. In the original language of the New Testament, Greek, this spiritual condition is summed up in the word *daimonizomai.* In various contemporary English translations the words used to describe this kind of influence or activities of demons over a person include *demoniac,* or *demon possessed.* Words such as *oppressed* and *suppressed* also are frequently used. More correctly, the phrase *"to be demonized"* is used to describe the spiritual condition of being under the influence or control of demons.

In any case, the Bible teaches that a person can come under demonic influence in various ways and to various degrees. Parts of a personality may come under the influence of demons, or an entire personality may be demonized.

The nature of demonic bondage is the subjection of the victim to a level of captivity whereby he or she loses his or her willpower, and therefore becomes an instrument or channel through which the particular operating demon(s) manifest and unleash their unclean and evil attitudes and activities. In terms of attitudes and activities, demons generally seek to dominate, control, and manipulate people, things, values, and the environment. It is through these broad activities that they initiate and maintain bondage. Anywhere control, manipulation, and domination exist, you can be sure demons are at work and that there are people who are, as a result, subjected to bondage. The Holy Spirit's plan is to bring believers through Christ into a position of dominion over demons. A believer should never aspire to exercise dominion over other believers, which amounts to domination and clearly is not of God. We are called to exercise dominion over Satan, his forces, and his activities.

Demonic bondage is a very broad subject, and as a result, I will attempt to explore its various dimensions by at least four approaches:

1. Demonic devices

2. Specific demonic behavioral activity

3. Specific biblical names of some demons

4. Demonic manifestation during deliverance minis-
   trations (this particular category is discussed in
   chapter 9)

Although these categories of activity are largely helpful in
identifying, describing, or diagnosing the presence of demons,
I do not necessarily suggest that a casual or occasional presence of one or two of the features listed in the next section
are sufficient to brand an individual as being "demonized,"
"oppressed," or "possessed." But a genuine concern about a
possible demonic presence or activity may be raised if the
following are true:

- There is a pattern of frequency of manifestation
  of the particular attitude or activity.

- There is a general feeling of spiritual and physical
  pressure or uneasiness on the part of the individual involved. This is often expressed as a lack
  of peace or inner stability or constant tension
  and fear.

- The pattern or severity of the activity remains
  intractable or worsens over time. In the case
  of a Christian believer not even the practice of
  repeated repenting, praying, fasting, counseling,
  and other biblical disciplinary steps can bring
  about any relief. In the same way the unbelieving
  sufferer never finds relief in the multitude of
  measures offered by clinicians, self-help coaches
  and gurus. Generally speaking, and for the most

part, demonic bondage may be elicited by the presence of a single or multiple sets of negative attitudes, behavior patterns, or actions on a consistent basis.

- Infrequent episodes of such attitudes, behavior patterns and actions may also indicate the influence of demons in an individual. The range of influence that demons exercise over their victims varies in severity and frequency. One of the simplest litmus tests that can be applied in determining whether a weakness is demonic or not is to ask the question, "Do I have the weakness or does the weakness have me?" Having the weakness means you can exercise control over it, and the weakness having you means it regularly exercises control over you to such an extent that you do things you would not normally do. And usually after such episodes, you are embarrassed, remorseful and yet helpless. In cases where the individual is completely under the control of demons such as in certain psychiatric states, he or she is usually oblivious to such actions and their consequences.

Demonic devices

There are at least six major devices that demons use in bringing people under their authority. Through these devices they succeed in domination, manipulation and control of their victims. Each of these devices reflects an aspect of the inherent nature and personality of Satan and demons. None of these activities can ever be attributable to the Holy Spirit; they are essentially attitudes and actions of evil spirits expressed through the corrupt and fallen nature in their victims.

1. Seduction/Deception: through the ministry of false prophets and false teachers, demons devise "doctrines" with which they draw people away from the truth and into error, "But the Spirit explicitly says that in the later times some will fall away from the faith, paying attention to deceitful spirits and doctrines of demons by means of the hypocrisy of liars seared in their own conscience as with a branding iron, men who forbid marriage and advocate abstaining from foods fully shared in by those who believe and know the truth" (1 Tim. 4:1–3).

Demonic deception includes, first, spiritual blindness whereby people are kept from believing the gospel (2 Cor. 4:3–4); and second, apostasy, a falling away from the truth, especially through strange laws and teachings about food and marriage, carnality, legalism, and damnable heresies (2 Thess. 2:3; 1 Tim. 4:1; 2 Pet. 2:1–2).

Notice that in 1 Timothy 4:1, it is the Holy Spirit who is referring to the other spirits as seductive or deceptive. He also reveals that these religious doctrines are authored by demons. When such demons gain access to the human heart, they blind the person's mind to truth and get them to believe lies, heresies, and counterfeits. In this way demons subject their victims under bondage and thus dominate and control them in their religious attitudes and actions.

2. Torment, Harassment, and Vexation: demons intensely torment and harass souls using a whole range of means such as fear, doubt, uncertainty, hopelessness, unbelief, terror, agitation, tension, perplexity, guilt, shame, condemnation, unworthiness, and sickness. None of these can be attributed to the Holy Spirit, which is the Spirit of love, peace, joy, and grace (Matt. 15:22; Luke 6:18; 1 Tim. 1:7; 1 John 4:18). The

Holy Spirit also gives soundness of mind and of body (Acts 3:16; 2 Tim. 1:7).

3. Compulsion/Drive: demons compel people to sin and commit negative evil actions against themselves and others. Some of the experiences indicative of demonic drive include restlessness, pressure, all forms of compulsive and addictive behaviors and attitudes, cursing, suicide, and homicide (Luke 8:29). Through the power of compulsion demons succeed in overwhelming their victims and keeping them in bondage.

4. Defilement: as unclean spirits, one of the primary jobs of demons is to impart unclean and foul thoughts, actions or life-styles such as lust, indecency, and dirty habits (e.g. smoking; immorality; obscene language, literature, or music; and other forms of pornography and blasphemy) (Matt. 10:1; Titus 1:15; Rev. 16:13).

5. Enticement: demons not only promote lust, the deviant and ungodly desires of the fallen (sinful) nature, but also set up the sinful opportunities or objects that gratify such lust. When the individual is so enticed, sin is accomplished, leading to death. Thus Satan uses demons to tempt individuals and bring them to sin (James 1:14).

6. Enslavement: demons seek to overrun people's minds and paralyze their resistance. Initially, this may start as a case of the individual yielding to an enticement or compulsion every once in a while until the spirit of slavery takes over (Rom. 8:15). This is the point where the individual becomes a spiritual slave and cannot help himself or herself by an act of decision or any other means. Deliverance at this point can only come through God's gracious, sovereign, supernatural power.

As a slave, the individual loses reason, discipline, decency and self-control. Depending on the nature of the weakness and degree of bondage, there is a progressive degeneration of the entire psychosocial and physical aspects, among others, of the total personality. In 1 Corinthians 6:12, Paul described this experience as being "brought under the power of." In other words, there is something beyond the control of the victim, a supernatural influence. And as long as the power or influence does not lead to the exercise of temperance or self control (for which the Holy Spirit is known) it is simply demonic.

Specific demonic behavioral patterns and activities

The human personality is composed of many parts, which are capable of healthy attitudes, actions, and relationships toward God and fellow humans. When these areas of the human personality are yielded to the Holy Spirit, such attitudes, actions, and relationships function in ways that promote personal stability, inner peace, or overall well being. The spirit, soul, and body therefore reach equilibrium, and only then will there be the necessary enhancement of healthy interpersonal relationship between the individual and others.

However, when these areas of personality are yielded to demons, there will be loss of inner peace, breakdown of personal stability, disruption of healthy interpersonal relationships, and any number of forms of emotional, mental, physical, and spiritual crises and frustrations. Demons bring about these crises when they enter the human personality and reside in the relevant areas of their specialty. When they thus secure their residence in some particular areas of the personality, they create a "neighborhood" over that area and proceed to dominate, control, and pervert the natural desires, longing, and activity of that area of the personality or body organ. The degree of havoc varies. Thus, some people who are demonically troubled in some areas of their personalities may still look normal, religious, respectable, and physically well-dressed, while others have outright abnormal traits, have "'no religion," and often blatantly express their primitive, demonic tendencies or instincts.

We will now consider some of the areas of the human personality that can be infested by demons. We will also list some demonic activities that can manifest in these areas.

1. Emotion: persistent fear, depression or heaviness (Isa. 61:3); mood swings; unexplainable sadness or moodiness; irritability; frequent outbursts of anger, rage, or wrath; suicidal thoughts; insanity; frequent thoughts of death; restlessness; excessive worry; incongruous affect; frequent and sometimes unexplainable weeping; fidgeting; nail biting; finger sucking (especially in adults); stress; persistent feelings of hopelessness; specific phobias; anxiety; frequent replay of bad memories; constant foreboding (of death, accident, or calamity); persistent guilt; condemnation; nervousness and panic; and sleeplessness.

Please bear in mind that not every episode of any of these emotional manifestations can be said to be demonic. Demonic involvement may be suspected if and when there is a pattern of frequency coupled with the fact that in most cases these are usually unexplainable by scientific or medical methods and unresponsive to basic spiritual and/or medical measures.

2. Attitudes: Persisting attitudes of unforgiveness, resentment, hatred, discrimination, racism, envy, rebellion, rejection, disappointment, despair, stubbornness, frustration, low self-esteem, self-pity, pride, superiority complexes, inferiority complexes, negative self image, persistent feeling of backwardness in life, actual manifestation of backwardness or failures in life endeavors, personal or family history of repeated or multiple break-up of marriage engagements and divorce, fear of mixing with other people, excessive worry or concern

over what other people think or fear of disapproval, cheating, and habitual traits of backbiting, shame, apathy, bitterness, criticism, jealousy, contention, domineering tendencies and manipulation, cruelty, cynicism, defeatism, aimlessness, and embarrassment.

3. The Mind: frequent patterns of confusion, compromise, frequent indecision or double mindedness, procrastination, doubt, unbelief, forgetfulness, and clouding of consciousness.

4. The Mouth (tongue or language): talkativeness, lying, cursing, obscene language, blasphemy, gossip, exaggeration, negative confession, enchantment, echolalia, (counterfeit of the New Testament gift of tongues), vulgarity, deceit, and false accusation.

5. The Will: all forms of addictive behavior (which mostly originates from the mind or emotion), including addiction to nicotine (smoking, chewing, or sniffing), alcohol and drugs, and addiction to naturally "good and useful" items or activities like caffeine, soft drinks, music, sleep, television, and food.

6. Sexuality: sex within the boundary of marriage is ordained by God and is good. However, sexual activities outside the confines of matrimony are illicit and sinful. Repeated indulgence in any form of illicit sexual activity or relationship is demonic. Common demonic sexuality may be described as extramarital, intramarital, and spirit-spouse sexual encounters.

a. Extramarital: the demon of lust is the primary demon behind all forms of illicit or pervert sexual behavior. It often manifests through adultery, fornication, voyeurism, exhibitionism, pornography, homosexuality/lesbianism, bisexuality, bestiality, incest, pedophilia and child sexual molestation, sadomasochism, use of sex trade articles, prostitution, fetishism, impure thoughts, masturbation, oral sex, rape, sexual fantasies, lewdness, nudity, transvestitism, seduction and enticement, inordinate affection, frequent wet dreams, and boasting about sexual powers or ability.

Opportunistic demons such as rebellion, witchcraft, compromise, materialism, violence, and even humanism lend their hands to help the demon of lust achieve its evil desire across the board of a wider society. These demons mount up pressure on the society even to the point of getting it to legitimize some of these perversions in the name of "civil rights" "or free speech" and thus labeling any meaningful opposition as discrimination and conservatism.

b. Intramarital: frequent tensions within marriages resulting from. alleged "excessive," "indiscriminate," or "repressed" sexual responses by one or both spouses may be demonic. Common examples include frigidity, fear of sex or fear of a spouse's legitimate sexual desire, "insatiable" or compulsive sexual appetites, perversions, domination or manipulation, constant romantic admiration of someone other than the spouse, constant attitude of preference for past (premarital) sexual relationship or preference of former sex partner to spouse, lack of sexual affection or attraction for spouse, masturbation, pornography, group sex, spousal swapping, and frequent baseless jealousy, suspicion or allegation of infidelity against spouse.

c. Spirit-spouse sexual encounters: this third category of demonic sexuality is what I call the "spirit-spouse" sexual encounter. It sounds incredible, but it is a real experience for countless numbers of men and women. In essence, this involves a direct sexual relationship between evil spirit beings and certain human beings. In our present age, this phenomenon has much to do with witchcraft, satanism, and the prevailing perverted sex culture. In most cases, many of the human victims of such violations were consciously involved in satanic sex rituals, prostitution, promiscuity, pornography, fornication, adultery, and other forms of perversions, and were therefore drawn into a covenant with a spirit-spouse. In some other cases through the use of witchcraft spells, some humans have been drawn into bondage to a spirit-spouse.

In its basic form, there is a pattern of sexual violation of the human partner by a demon. Common scenarios include frequent erotic dreams, during which certain demons assume the image of someone (of the same or opposite sex) known to the victim. In some cases, the experience becomes frequent to the extent that the demon assumes the status of a spouse—a spirit-spouse, as it is known in some circles. This spirit-spouse can operate even when its human partner has a legitimate human spouse. In some literature or circles, at least two kinds of demons have been identified as an incubus (a male demon) or a succubus (a female demon). Both of these spirits are said to regularly violate humans of the opposite sex. Such encounters mostly occur in dreams; however, some victims have also reported experiences of this kind while awake.

Some of these demons also torment their victims with conflicts and confusion about their sexual identity, leading to homosexuality and other forms of sexual perversion. Other common results in the victim may include gratification or pleasure, while some may experience fear, nightmares, weakness, guilt, disgust, and feelings of defilement and shame. In extreme situations, consequences may include the victim's failure to get married in the physical realm. Where such victims prevail and get married, barrenness or frequent miscarriages, marital tensions, and divorce are prevalent. These demons through their possessive and competitive attitudes and actions frequently frustrate real life marital relationships, pregnancy, and child-bearing.

In various third world cultures, especially in cases where the gospel of Jesus Christ is not received, many victims do get into real life marital covenants with such spirit-spouses through elaborate wedding ceremonies. In parts of Africa, these are known as water spirits because they live mostly in rivers. They are also known as mermaid spirits or "mammy water spirits." Similar covenant spirits include *Ogbanje* and *Abiku* spirits. In the course of my ministry, I have encountered these spirits among a great number of westerners and have come to a conclusion that, like many other forms of spiritual problems, this is a universal one. The way out is to break or renounce any pact or covenant with such demons.

These forms of bizarre contemporary sexual relationship between humans and spirit beings has an antediluvian parallel in which a certain group of angels left their realm to cohabit and have sexual intercourse with human women. This was first documented in the Book of Genesis, "Now it came about, when men began to multiply on the face of the land and daughters were born to them, that the sons of God (angels in this context) saw that the daughters of men were beautiful, they took wives for themselves, whomsoever they chose" (Gen. 6:1–2).

The fruit of such relationship was also documented in these words, "The Nephilim were on the earth in those days and also afterward, when the sons of God came in to the daughters of men and they bore children to them. Those were the mighty men who were of old, men of renown" (Gen. 6:4). This verse is a most clear description of such sexual intercourse between spirit beings and earthly women. Apparently, God's judgment was riot restrained from visiting such awful wickedness. In fact, it is generally believed that these angels are referred to in the Book of Jude verse 6 as those who "did not keep their own domain and abandoned their proper abode." And on an additional note, if Jesus did draw strong points of similarities between the days of Noah, when these things happened, and this present age, there is no question therefore that such perversion is also possible now (Luke 17:26).

7. The Human Spirit: having considered the various activities of demons in the mind and emotion of people, it is not an overstatement to say that since demons are spirit beings, they tend to be even more at home in the spirit of their victims. Some of the common demonic activities that can be manifested through the human spirit are strange spiritual phenomena, dream patterns, and religious activity.

a. Strange spiritual phenomena: clairvoyance; hallucinations; persistent strange negative inner voice(s); false "revelations;" telepathy; occult based predictions; frequent feelings of a strange or eerie presence resulting in fear, trembling, heaviness, light-headedness, tension or discomfort, and sometimes euphoria; frequent unexplainable acquisition of money or certain items (e.g. bangles, rings, clothing, etc.); frequent unexplainable loss of personal money or items including valuables such as wedding rings; specific extreme phobias of water, insects, darkness, heights, etc., especially in adults; and negative reactions to the name of Jesus Christ or prayer manifesting as opposition, mockery, fear, shivering, shaking, or screaming.

b. Dream patterns: frequent occurrence of being pressed down in sleep to the point of inability to speak or breathe; very deep sleep patterns; a pattern of forgetfulness of dreams; nightmares (especially pursuit by snakes, dogs, cats, or other horror figures); dreams of wandering in cemeteries, forests and other forms of desolate places, attending covens, swimming, flying, floating in the air, and eating among strangers; and frequent dream episodes of sexual intercourse, pregnancy, childbearing, or miscarriages, which often result in real life miscarriages or infertility.

c. Religious activity: religious activity is a very significant aspect of human spirituality. However, not all religious attitude or activity is from God. And religious spirits constitute the most active, deceptive, and destructive type of demons. Some of the specific personal or group activities attributable to religious spirits include domination or control, witchcraft, blasphemy, strife, contention, jealousy, criticism, unforgiveness, manipulation (especially "church politics"), judging, backbiting, division, pride, unbelief, doubt, self-righteousness, poverty, gossip, deception, heresies, false prophets, false teachers, tradition, obsession with religious titles and positions, spirit of anti-Christ (another Jesus, another gospel, another spirit syndrome), legalism, carnality, obsessive focus on objects and methods of worship and programs, cultism, occultism, idolatry, new age practices, syncretism, hypocrisy, murder, and terrorism.

Generally, the following attitudes and beliefs readily indicate the influence of religious demons at work in individuals and religious groups:

- Denial of the deity and divinity of Jesus Christ as Messiah
- Denial of the persons and relationship between the persons of the Godhead
- Denial of the finished work of Jesus Christ on the cross and His resurrection as the sole basis for salvation

- Elevation of certain church or denominational leaders to the level ascribed to the Lord Jesus Christ

- Focusing worship on the various means of appropriating grace, such as worship forms or styles, Eucharist or communion, liturgies, spiritual gifts, "anointing," and fruits of the Spirit instead of the Lord Himself

- Elevation of church traditions, writings, and doctrines to the same level of importance, authority or even infallibility as God's Word (the sixty-six books of Old Testament and New Testament)

- Gullible acceptance of every form of religious activity without exercising necessary biblical discernment (Eph. 4:14; 2 Thess. 2:7–12; 1 John 4:1)

- Outright rejection of a genuine scriptural religious experience for fear of losing the status quo or age long religious traditions (2 Tim. 2:16; 3:5, 13)

- An arrogant belief by membership of the exclusive correctness of their local congregation, denomination, or movement, and a labeling of "error" on other groups or movements

- A leadership that demands an unquestioned acceptance of its teaching, doctrine, leadership styles, rites, and forms or formulas of worship insistence on the observance of religious laws, days or festivals as a means of achieving righteousness, e.g. vegetarianism, keeping of Sabbaths, new moon ordinances, worship of angels, human traditions, celibacy, philosophies, etc. (Col. 2:8–16; 1 Tim. 1:6; 6:5)

- Turning back to past non-biblical and vain religious practices and as a result yielding again to bondage to elemental spirits (Gal. 2:4; 3:1; 4:9–10)

- Admittance of false teachers and prophets, who lead the people into sin with their doctrines or teachings (2 Pet. 2:1–18; Rev. 2:12–16, 18–22)

Generally, in such religious circles, faith, revelation, anointing, and the Person of the Holy Spirit are relegated to secondary or tertiary importance, if at all. Usually theology, reason, eloquence, and social programs become cornerstone features in such groups. Psychology, sociology, and science become the major or only means of solving life's problems, including spiritual needs, and the person and gifts of the Holy Spirit thus have no relevance in the personal and corporate life of the group.

8. The body: demons can and do attack the human body in the same way that they attack the spirit and the soul. In fact, a great deal of demonic manifestation in a human life is mediated through the body. Many of the physical phenomena we may be considering are not explainable scientifically or medically. Certain of these conditions are, to some extent, explainable but may or may not completely submit to medical remedies. In any case, these conditions submit to prayer exercised in faith in the name of the Lord Jesus Christ. Most of the medical or health problems indicating the presence and activity of demons are:

- generational or inherited
- chronic in their course
- defiant to psychological counseling and medical treatment
- without definitive scientifically identified causative entity or process (Some do have definitive causes but do not respond to treatment.)

Up to the present century, medical science does not supply satisfactory answers to the cause, course or treatment of many medical problems. In many cases when it does provide insight to the causes, it does not provide a lasting remedy. In such instances, the victim is left only to one choice: namely, expensive lifetime conservative or palliative treatment. One of such sufferer was described in these words, "And a woman who had a hemorrhage for twelve years and had endured much at the hands of many physicians and had spent all that she had and was not helped at all but rather had grown worse" (Mark 5:25–26).

This woman in question could not get relief from this chronic form of hemorrhage after seeking help from many physicians and enduring all the distress and difficulties associated with getting the best of scientific medicine. Moreover, it was a very expensive venture, as it still is today. Having made the best of her human efforts, she came to the end of herself and sought spiritual help for an apparently physical medical problem, receiving healing instantly and permanently through her personal faith in Jesus Christ (Mark 5:27–34).

Spirit of infirmity

Most physical and psychosomatic illnesses are demonic in origin. A psychosomatic illness is one whose cause is the result of the interplay of forces upsetting the balance between the mind (psyche) and the body (soma), hence the term *psychosomatic*. In any case, during His ministry the Lord Jesus often encountered many people who were victims of apparently physical ailments. Despite the outward manifestation of physical symptoms, He often identified specific demons responsible for them with great discernment and to the amazement of onlookers. He proceeded to rebuke and cast such spirits of infirmity out of the diseased body, resulting in physical healing.

A particular case in point was that of another invalid described in the Book of Luke:

> And, behold, there was a woman who had a spirit
> of infirmity eighteen years, and was bowed together
> and could in no wise lift up herself.
>
> —LUKE 13:11

It is a clear fact that this woman's ailment was physical, a kind of spinal or back problem. However, the Lord discerned a "spirit of infirmity" as the cause. She had endured this torment for eighteen years, probably because the ailment had been misdiagnosed as a mere physical problem. Furthermore, the Lord proceeded to heal her by inviting her to Himself and declaring her healed, having laid hands on her. Her healing was instantaneous, miraculous, and glorified God (Luke 13:12–13).

In response to the attitude and protest of the religious leaders present, the Lord shed more light on the situation by pointing out the following helpful truths. First, this woman was a daughter of Abraham, a natural descendant of Abraham and an heir of God's promises to Abraham including health and healing. Second, it was Satan who bound or afflicted this woman through the activity of a spirit or demon of infirmity

119

(Acts 10:38; Luke 13:12–13). Third, Jesus and His disciples have a divine mandate to undo all the evil Satan and his servants had dealt on humanity including sickness. Fourth, it is not God's will for anyone to deny the power of Christ and remain in bondage. Moreover, any form of opposition to genuine healing and deliverance of people from the power of the enemy is hypocrisy and unscriptural. Just as that woman had remained bound for eighteen years and had been a worshiper in that synagogue during those years of bondage, many Christians have been in church all their lives and have remained bound. In many cases, as in the case of this particular synagogue, legalism sustains ignorance and bondage.

Another incident in the New Testament that buttresses the fact that a spirit of infirmity brings about physical illness, defects, handicap, or disease in a human life is recorded in Mark 9:17–27. In this incident, a father brought his child who was deaf and dumb. No gainsaying, deafness and dumbness are apparently physical in nature, and there is sufficient scientific and medical explanation for both conditions. However, both the boy's father and the Lord discerned a demon at work; the demon also generated other physical symptoms in this boy including gnashing and clenching of the teeth, foaming from the mouth, body stiffness, falling to the ground, convulsion, and crying. Moreover, Jesus not only identified a demon but also dealt with the spirit as a person and by name. By referring to the spirit as a "deaf and dumb spirit," Jesus clearly implies that this particular case and many other conditions of deafness and dumbness are demonic in origin.

The fact that the Lord, in dealing with diseases, identified a demon as the root cause and decisively dealt with that spirit in order to procure an effective and lasting healing and deliverance is highly instructive. It suggests the fact that the spirit of infirmity is the life force sustaining the sickness or disease. As long as this spirit remains alive and embedded in the individual, the disease remains active in that individual's physical body. However, when this spirit of infirmity is confronted under the anointing of the Holy Spirit and in the name of the Lord Jesus Christ with the Word of God, this demon is expelled, healing of the body results, and God is glorified.

The following is a listing of some of the physical and psychosomatic disease conditions attributable to demons. They are categorized according to body systems.

1. Emotional: neuroses, anxiety, nervousness, obsessive compulsive behavior and disorders, panic states, phobias, paranoia, and paranoid states, addictive behaviors, depression, mania, manic depressive disorders, insomnia, dementia, Alzheimer's and other confused states, palsies, bedwetting, and psychosis (insanity), e.g. schizophrenia.

2. Neurological: blindness, visual defects, cataracts, glaucoma, mutism, dumbness, crossed eyes, seizure disorders (epilepsy or convulsions), chronic dizziness, numbness of extremities, mongolism, Parkinson's disease, loss of positional balance, and speech defects, e.g. stammering.

3. Respiratory: sinusitis, foul breath, asthma, shortness of breath, emphysema.

4. Skin: acne, psoriasis, skin cancer, eczema, moles and warts, some forms of body odor, and itches.

5. Immunological and Connective Tissue: allergies, lupus, arthritis, gout, leukemia, multiple sclerosis, kidney defects, and infections.

6. Cardiovascular: varicose veins, chest pains, heart attacks, thrombosis, heart diseases and congenital defects, palpitations and fainting, chronic severe weakness, lethargy, blood diseases, sickle cell anemia, angina, hypertension.

7. Gastrointestinal Metabolic: ulcers, cancer, hemorrhoids, digestive problems, diabetes, obesity, cramps, pain, inflammations, stones, gallbladder problems, tumors, frequent nausea, hernias, goiters, and heartburn.

8. Musculoskeletal: back pains, joint pains, arthritis, myasthenia, gravis, unequal legs, paralysis, muscle wasting, spinal curvatures, spinal defects, shoulder pains, cramps, spasms, muscular dystrophy, withered extremities, bone and tissue cancer, ingrown toenails.

9. Genitourinary: cancer, inflammations, stones, and infection and bleeding in the kidneys, bladder, uterus, and urethras.

10. Reproductive: male impotence, torsion, congenital defects, tumors and cancers, barrenness (primary infertility), secondary infertility, and frequent miscarriages. Caution!

We must not minimize the value or relevance of modern medicine and psychology. However, each case must be approached with the leading of the Holy Spirit and also in due consideration of the faith of the person receiving ministry. Although the word is not opposed to modern medicine, it clearly shows that God has made divine provision for the healing of His people through faith in the name of Jesus Christ. Therefore, caution must be exercised in determining the need for the discontinuation of medical therapy or otherwise without a consideration of the faith of the patient for divine healing and deliverance. It is important to first build up the faith of the one seeking healing. This is best done by sound biblical teaching and proclamation of the gospel of the cross. Generally, diseases and sicknesses are essentially one of the results of the Fall of Adam and an aspect of the curse of the broken law upon humanity. Through these disease conditions, demons seek to exercise dominion over the physical body.

The Fall brought about corruption in the physical body, and one of the manifestations of this corruption is disease. Ultimately, this corruption expressed through disease results in mortality in the physical body: God in His wisdom has a wonderful eternal plan for our mortal bodies. This plan is "immortality" at the rapture (1 Cor. 15:54, 56–58). However, in the interim before the resurrection and the rapture, God in His love through Jesus Christ offers us divine health and healing in this present age by the quickening of our mortal bodies through the Holy Spirit (Rom. 8:11). In this way, Satan and his demons cease to have dominion over the human body.

Even if there is some uncertainty as to whether a disease is demonic in its origin or not, we need to be reassured that our God, Jehovah Rapha, which means the Lord our healer, heals all manner of diseases and sicknesses (Exodus 15:26; Matt. 10:1). As we have already observed, even in the earthly ministry of Jesus, there were healings that did not necessitate the casting out of demons.

Specific Biblical Names and Activities of Some Demons

One of the most effective means of understanding demonic bondage is by exploring the various names given to some specific demons in the Bible. Many evil spirits or demons are referred to by specific names in the Bible. These names reveal the exact nature, function or activity of the particular demon so named.

Some of the demons addressed by specific names in the Bible include the following:

- spirit of the world (1 Cor. 2:12)
- spirit of divination (fortune telling) (Acts 16:16)
- spirit of harlotry (Hos. 4:12–13)
- spirit of impurity (Zech. 13:2)
- spirit of jealousy (Num. 5:14–30)
- spirit of stress/distress/terror (1 Sam. 16:4–23)
- spirit of despair/hopelessness, heaviness (depression) (Isa. 61:3)
- spirit of slumber/sleep (Isa. 29:10)
- spirit of fear and timidity (2 Tim. 1:7)
- spirit of deafness/dumbness (Mark 9:25)
- spirit of muteness (Mark 9:7–17)
- spirit of infirmity (sickness) (Luke 13:11)
- spirit of deception/error (1 Tim. 4:1; 1 John 4:6)
- lying spirit (1 Kings 22:22; 2 Chronicles 18:20–22)
- evil wish (treachery, deceit) (Judges 9:23)

There is a strong demonstration that the activities listed after the word *spirit* in each case are demonic and not mere character or personality weaknesses or failures.

Naturally, there is a tendency to consider or diagnose the above problems as merely emotional, psychological or physical problems; however, in a majority of cases, scripture and experience show these are results of demonic activity. It may be correct to say that these were initially the results of emotional, psychological or physical weaknesses; but over a certain period of time, the door is opened for the relevant, demons to come in and systematically entrench the particular activity, weakness or perversion in question.

8

RELEASE TO THE CAPTIVES

O NE VITAL ASPECT of salvation is our freedom from the claims, authority, and indwelling presence of demons. Deliverance from demons is an integral component of God's salvation package. The Bible documents God's many promises concerning our deliverance from the indwelling presence and power of evil spirits. Two of the most popular of these promises are found in the prophecies of Obadiah and Joel:

> But upon Mount Zion shall be deliverance, and there shall be holiness; and the house of Jacob shall possess their possession.
>
> —OBADIAH 1:7, 1

> And it shall come to pass, that whosoever shall call on the name of the Lord shall be delivered: for in Mount Zion and in Jerusalem shall be deliverance, as the Lord had said, in the remnant whom the Lord shall call.
>
> —JOEL 2:32, 1

In fact, God's promises of deliverance date as far back as His infallible covenant with Abraham, His servant. On the basis of this covenant, salvation—including forgiveness of sins, healing of diseases, and deliverance from demons—is graciously released to all who would believe the gospel of Jesus Christ. Almighty God has indeed committed Himself by an oath to save, heal, deliver and materially prosper believers. This plan of total salvation was revealed through the prophets and executed in the Lord Jesus Christ by the Holy Spirit on the cross (Luke 1:68–73). Zechariah the priest acknowledged this grace at the dedication of his son John the Baptist in the following words, "The oath which He (God) swore to Abraham our father, to grant us that we, being delivered from the hand of our enemies, might serve Him without fear in holiness and righteousness before Him all our days" (Luke 1:73–75).

This prophecy reveals some practical lessons, which include the facts that demons are our enemies and hate us with a grave hatred. When they have us under their dominion, they torment us with fear, sickness, and sin, working tirelessly to keep us from God's righteousness and holiness. On the other hand, God wants us to serve Him without fear and to walk in holiness and righteousness for the rest of our lives. When the Lord Jesus Christ, God's horn of salvation, came (Luke 1:29), He executed this covenant of deliverance by His finished work on the cross; and after His resurrection from the dead, He also commissioned His followers to continue to expel demons from the lives of all who believe in Him, thereafter keeping demons under subjection (Mark 16:14–20). The divine provision of deliverance from evil spirits is no longer a future expectation but a present reality. The church now has a mandate and anointing from the Lord to effectively challenge demons, cast them out of people's lives, and keep them under subjection.

Everyone who is under demonic influence or bondage but receives the gospel of the kingdom and believes in the Lord Jesus Christ as savior and deliverer will not only be set be set free but go on to walk in dominion over demons. The covenant is not only about being free from demons but also about treading upon them and keeping them under subjection in the name of the Lord Jesus. This covenant of deliverance is an invaluable divine authority in the hand of the church. This truth is known to and obeyed by Satan, demons, and other satanic agents. However, many Christians are either ignorant of it or are reluctant to execute it for reasons including doubt, unbelief, fear, or theological prejudice.

COME OUT OF HIM

There is no one singular method by which deliverance may be ministered. The only standard to which believers should look is the standard set by the Lord Himself and adopted by the early church. Often some people receive deliverance in unexpected places and at unusual times. Sometimes, just as in the case of the man in the synagogue in Capernaum, some people get delivered while the Word of God is being preached or taught (Mark 1:21–27). At other times, people have obtained deliverance during a praise and worship session. The term *self-deliverance* is used by some to refer to situations whereby some people who recognize the presence and activity of demons in their lives proceed to repent and confess the sins that opened the door for those demons, forgiving those who hurt them, renouncing all points of demonic contacts in their lives, and expelling the demons in the name of Jesus.

Mass deliverance is a common component and feature of most evangelistic "crusade" or revival meetings dealing with large groups of people where it is impossible to counsel, lay hands on, and pray individually for all persons who need deliverance from evil spirits. Small group deliverance ministration, on the other hand, is one of the most effective but time-consuming and demanding methods. It usually involves interviewing, counseling, teaching, and prayer of deliverance. Small groups may mean one-on-one sessions or sessions involving more than one person in need of deliverance.

There are also many formats in use by various Christian workers involved in the ministry of deliverance. However, we need to realize that no one format or method can claim superiority over others. What is important is that such methods and teachings are in line with the method of Jesus Christ and the early church. The renewed emphasis on the ministry of deliverance and other aspects of "power evangelism" demands a great deal of discernment, as there are overzealous people who are out to exploit victims for some selfish ends. Moreover, new age, non-Christian exorcists and other false prophets are also lying in wait to entice desperate seekers.

SUGGESTED STEPS TO DELIVERANCE

The following is a suggested series of steps to deliverance from demons. These steps are not a set of doctrines. They are also modifiable to suit the particular setting, situation, or size of group receiving ministry. These are not a set of dogma but are some helpful guidelines based on basic and tested principles of the Bible. Furthermore, these steps are to be undertaken by the person seeking freedom. The one ministering the deliverance only leads under the direction of the Holy Spirit. These steps are also applicable to "self deliverance" as well as large group sessions.

1. Come to the Lord and Savior Jesus Christ

Acknowledge Jesus Christ as God's begotten Son and the only way to God. Declare your personal faith in Him for salvation and deliverance. This faith is exercised by believing these facts in your heart and confessing them with your mouth (Heb.

3:1; Matt. 11:28; John 6:37; Rom. 10:9–10). By these acts of faith, Jesus is invited as Lord to exercise ownership over you.

2. Repent

Acknowledge, confess, and repent every known personal or ancestral sin. Failure to confess sins hinders fellowship between God and humans and opens us up to demonic oppressions, judgment, and other forms of adversities. However, confession of sins and repentance restores fellowship and God's mercy. In many situations, apart from confessing to God, there may be need to also confess to other people our wrong attitudes or actions toward them (Exod. 20:1–5; Prov. 28:13; John 1:9). It is through repentance that we receive God's forgiveness and justification. This opens the door for God's mercy and grace into our lives.

3. Denounce and renounce

Denounce and renounce all ancestral and personal involvement in evil covenants, idolatry, cult involvements, occult contacts, addictive habits, sinful habits, and besetting sins. When this is done in faith by a decision of the will and expressed in verbal declarations, it constitutes a deliberate reversal of any known wrong actions (Deut. 7:26; Isa. 55:7; Acts 19:13–19; Eph. 5:11–12). Tolerating or accommodating all known evil objects, contacts, practices or actions as listed above offers sufficient grounds and open doors for demons to continue to torment their victims. Through the act of denunciation the victim takes his or her stand with God in condemning whatever evil he or she was involved in. In this way the person gets to condemn what God condemns. This is indeed hating those who hate God: Satan, his demons, principalities, and their objects, articles and practices. Hating such enemies of God is a very important prerequisite for deliverance from demons (Ps. 139:20–21).

Renunciation, on the other hand, closes the door, neutralizing every legal claim held by demons for continued oppression. Renunciation burns the bridge to the victim's evil past. Through renunciation, the victim notifies the demons about the termination of their tenancy in his or her life. In fact, he or she revokes the lease of the tenancy agreement through the spiritual act known as renunciation. After this initial renunciation, the believer can go on and renounce all significant contacts with evil as they surface to memory. This may be an ongoing exercise. Renunciation also signifies the victim's commitment to change his or her evil ways. It is also a personal decision to cease or withdraw all involvement in or association with the denounced person, attitude or act. When done with simple faith, renunciation is a very effective step to deliverance. It usually marks a turning point in the course of deliverance.

4. Identify with Christ

Acknowledge by faith in your heart the *substitutionary* suffering, death on the cross, burial, and resurrection of Jesus Christ from the dead, and recognize these as the basis for salvation and deliverance (John 12:31, Heb. 10:14). Furthermore, in identifying with Christ, you also need to acknowledge your co-death with Christ. In other words, not only did He die in your place but that He also included you in Himself when He died and when He was raised from death (2 Cor. 5:14–15). Our death and resurrection with Christ justifies us from sin and all satanic power (Rom. 4:25). Therefore, identification with Christ in this way should be an abiding attitude in the believer before and after deliverance from demons.

5. Proclaim

Proclaim the power, accomplishments, and benefits of the cross and the blood of Jesus Christ over your life. Testify of

Christ's victory by His shed blood on the cross over Satan and his forces in your life (Rom. 5:9; 1 Cor. 6:19; Eph. 1:7; Col. 2:14–15; Heb. 13:12; 1 John 1:9; Rev. 12:11).

6. Forgive

Forgive those who have hurt you. Ask the Holy Spirit to pour out His forgiving grace upon your heart (Matt. 18:23–35; Mark 11:25–26; Rom. 5:5).

7. Revoke

Revoke every ancestral (generational), personal and any other form of curse at work in your life, knowing that the Lord has redeemed you, the believer, from them and had authorized you to cancel them (Matt. 18:18–20; Gal. 3:14–15).

8. Bind

By word of command, bind all evil forces at work in your life in the name of Jesus Christ (Matt. 16:16–19; 18:18–20; Phil. 2:10–11).

9. Say a prayer of denunciation and renunciation

Steps 1–8 are not just empty religious exercise but are indeed a blend of right spiritual attitudes and divine facts based on biblical revelation. More importantly, when believed in the heart and confessed with the mouth, such a declaration of faith and prayer is invariably a most potent and efficacious weapon to dislodge demons from their trenches in the human body. Essentially, this act of faith is the victim's personal assertion of his or her freedom in Christ. Usually, the person ministering deliverance leads the one being prayed for through a short prayer reflecting the basic elements of the attitudes and facts listed in steps 1–8. This is not a magical formula because if not done in faith it is powerless. It is only an expression or declaration of faith.

In my personal experience over many years of ministering deliverance, I have observed that this is the most decisive moment both for the recipient of deliverance and for the demons in the person. Many forms of reaction and opposition suddenly surface at this stage, common among which are these:

- refusal of the recipient to complete the prayer
- refusal to mention the name of Jesus, His blood, cross, or lordship, either through a sudden loss of voice or deliberate refusal to say the words
- physical reactions such as choking, coughing, and retching; various kinds of body sensations, especially in the abdomen or stomach area; shouting; and yelling, etc.
- falling, kicking, and struggling
- verbal opposition to God, the Lord Jesus, and His finished work, the church, or the one ministering deliverance

10. Say a prayer of authority

Having led the one in need of deliverance in prayer of renunciation, the minister then proceeds to evict or expel the offending demons by a prayer of authority. In the case of deliverance from demons, the prayer of authority is based on faith in the finished work of the Lord Jesus as revealed in God's Word. This prayer is essentially a command issued in faith and in the name of the Lord Jesus and demands that every demon leave its victim(s). This is the divine quit notice served or administered by the Lord's minister. When the prayer is issued in faith and on the basis of the Lord's finished work and His name, every demon at work or referred to by name or function must bow and yield.

Since some demons may initially bluff by way of delayed manifestation or delayed exit, the minister in this case must not entertain negative emotions such as doubt, fear, discouragement, or impatience. He or she must continue to stand in faith on the ground of the finished work and the Lord's name, knowing that the demons have heard this command, and stand by his or her command based on God's Word, which says, "In My name they shall cast out demons," and never on his or her own merits or demerits. Refuse bluff, manipulation, and intimidation.

Remember, the prayer of renunciation by the one in need of deliverance tears the "lease agreement" with demons, whereas the prayer of authority by the minister is the "divine eviction order" served by an agent of God's kingdom (Eccl. 8:4; Mark 16:17; Luke 10:17–18). The prayer of authority must be precise, clear and direct. When laced with scriptures, these commands are much more divinely potentiated and exert a much more lacerating effect on demons. Remember God's Word is the sword of the Spirit (Eph. 6:17). Ultimately, these demand that demons come out of their victims (Mark 1:25; 5:8; Acts 16:18). The prayer of authority is never addressed to the person being prayed for but to the demon in him or her. In cases where more than one person is ministering deliverance, it is recommended that one person take the lead to issue the commands while the others pray in agreement. Orders from more than one person at the same time may be conflicting and counterproductive, as the demons get confused. Effective spiritual authority must reflect unity because "a house divided against itself shall not stand" (Matt. 12:25).

In the case of self-deliverance, the one in need of deliverance by himself or herself proceeds with a prayer of authority after he or she has made a prayer of renunciation.

11. Be filled

Invite the Holy Spirit to fill the person delivered and instruct him or her to receive the Holy Spirit by faith. If he or she has previously received the baptism of the Holy Spirit, encourage him or her to seek regular infillings and to acknowledge on a regular basis the indwelling presence of the Holy Spirit in his or her personal life.

12. Spend time

It is vital to spend time in thanksgiving, praise and worship with a triumphant attitude.

13. Follow-up

Take refuge in scriptures, devotion, prayer, praise, Bible study, counseling, and fellowship, especially within the first two weeks after initial ministering.

Again, it is important to note that these steps are not a set of doctrines or a magical formula in themselves. We must acknowledge deliverance as a gift from almighty God only administered to us by the Holy Spirit on the basis of faith in Jesus Christ and His finished work on the cross.

MANIFESTATION

During deliverance sessions, most demons reveal their nature, name, character, activity, and exit route by certain forms of physical expressions through the various parts of the body of the person receiving deliverance. Sometimes, these manifestations also reveal the stage, prognosis or progress of the course of the deliverance. Essentially, these manifestations are reactions of the invisible demons revealed through the visible body parts of their victim. This is just in the same way that the sovereign, invisible Lord—the Holy Spirit—manifests Himself in the lives and bodies of believers in Jesus Christ through His fruit and gifts.

On the basis of scriptural revelation and personal ministry experience, I want to list some of the most commonly occurring manifestations. I would like to deal with these manifestations along the lines of the various parts of the body and human personality where they occur the most.

1. The Mouth: In both the Hebrew and Greek original languages of the Old Testament and New Testament respectively, the word for spirit is the word for breath. Whereas the Holy Spirit is the breath of almighty God (Ps. 33:6), demons or evil spirits are the breath of Satan. Generally, both breath and spirits are invisible. The mouth and the entire human airway apparatus is a major channel of passage for spirits. Most manifestations during deliverance sessions occur around the mouth or airway. Such manifestations include coughing, sneezing, choking, belching, hiccups, spitting, vomiting, long and repeated yawns, and panting or fast breathing. Also included are clenching of teeth, gagging, and varying sensations in the throat, such as pressure, crawling, dryness, or obstruction. Drooling and copious salivation may also be observed.

2. The Trunk and Extremities: Based on Mark 9:17–26, the following symptoms may be observed in the trunk and extremities of the body: stiffness, wriggling, itching, flexion, extension, dancing, struggling, kicking, fighting, biting, hitting, twitches, convulsions, twisting, rotation of head and neck, spinning, finger stiffness, facial twitches, feeling of mild burning sensation or intense heat or cold, headaches, snake-like motions, jerking, or feeling of mild or intense pain or tugging in certain parts of the body, especially abdomen, chest, back, extremities, and loins. A bearing down sensation that is very similar to that experienced by laboring women

during childbirth may occur. In some cases, such labor-like sensations also culminate in "delivery" of demons especially through the passing of gases or fluids or by a mere feeling of "something left me or came out of me."

3. Eyes: glazed eyes, tears, eyeball fixation, closed eyelids, upwards or sideward rolling of the eyeballs, focused gaze (at a person, an object or empty space), covering of eyes with hands, or facial expressions of anger or pain.

4. Posture: running, stooping, bending, falling down on the back or side followed by crawling, sitting up, kicking, or a corpse-like posture (Mark 9:26, Acts 8:7).

5. The Emotion: anger, resentment, quarrelling, cursing, blasphemies, threats, stubbornness, shyness, violence, rage, resistance, boasting, quietness, secretiveness, disorientation, or argument.

6. The Spirit: demons sometimes emit foul odors and speak in strange voices during deliverance sessions. Such manifestations make the immediate presence of such demons more vivid. Often such voices are hoarse and deep, and in most cases different from the normal voice of the victim. Generally speaking, demons utter resistance, intimidation, lies and false claims, threats of retaliation, fear, profanity, and sometimes laughter or cries.

"Falling Under the Power" or "Slain in the Spirit"

Demons do fall down with their victims during deliverance and healing sessions. Such manifestations are not only common in contemporary experience but were also evident in the ministry of the Lord and in that of the early church. A typical scenario was recorded in the Gospel of Mark, "And He told His disciples that a boat should stand ready for Him because of the multitude, in order that they might not crowd Him; for He had healed many, with the result that all those who had afflictions pressed about Him in other to touch Him. And whenever the unclean spirits beheld Him, they would fall down before Him and cry out, saying, 'You are the son of God!'" (Mark 3:9–11). However, falling down during prayer or ministry, as well as laughing, is not always due to demonic activity. The presence of the Holy Spirit also can lead to falling, laughing, and other phenomena. Falling may also be attributable to other factors. However, it is not within the scope of this work to fully discuss the phenomenon of "falling under the power."

Generally, when demons are challenged in the name of the Lord Jesus Christ and by the power of the Holy Spirit, they come under intense torment and are forced to seek emergency exit. They do manifest in the process. However, some demons choose to leave their victims quietly. The absence of manifestations during ministration does not necessarily indicate an abortive ministration. Also, the presence of manifestations does not necessarily indicate successful ministration. In most cases of deliverance, instant relief is obtained to some extent or completely, whereas in other cases relief is obtained only after a series of sessions.

SIGNS OF RELEASE

Release is not always easy to determine because of various reasons. First, some relief may be instant while some is gradual, needing considerable follow-up. Second, some forms of instant relief don't necessarily mean lasting freedom. In any case, early signs of relief may include:

- a feeling of ease as uneasiness lifts

- a feeling of lightness as a sense of burden or heaviness lifts, (most times the victim feels like a massive ton of weight has been removed)

- disappearance of pressure, tension or fear

- general deep sense of joy, peace, satisfaction, purity and freedom

- a sense of brokenness, amazement, thanksgiving, and praise

- a deep sense of repentance from evil attitudes and involvement in wrong relationship and activities or specific sins

- a deep hunger for righteousness and fellowship with the light of Jesus Christ

- healing of emotional and physical infirmities, as well as other miracles

- a rekindled prayer life (a common sequel in the first two weeks following an effective ministration.)

- the relief of the specific symptom(s) of bondage or demonic activity that necessitated the ministering of deliverance (These may not often be instantaneous. Some release maybe gradual. In most cases, the difference between an instantaneous or gradual outcome or even a persistence of symptoms is dependent on the faith of the person prayed for. If the recipient of ministry continues in unbelief, doubt, hopelessness, fear, and ignorance of the power of the word and the cross, the experience of real freedom will remain elusive. However, if in the face of bluff by demons and persistent symptoms the person

receiving prayer takes a final stand on the facts
of God's Word and reckons with Satan's defeat
on the cross, rejecting doubt, hopelessness, and
fear, the offending demons inevitably get worn
out. This is the faith that overcomes—an attitude that will not retreat from the truth of the
finished work of the cross and the resultant
powerlessness of Satan and his cohorts.)

We must remember that ultimately, a successful deliverance
experience may not mean an immediate cessation of every
problem in our lives. But if through the ministry of deliverance
we come to a point where we regain boldness to say no to the
voice or pressure from the offending demon(s) and proceed to
serve God without fear but in holiness, then the specific release
or blessing we are seeking will be "added unto us" (Matt. 6:33).
Then we know we have sought and found His kingdom and His
righteousness. This is the Mount Zion experience where we as
God's people receive deliverance and come under His holiness
(Obad. 1:7). This is our freedom in Christ. In this way we are
free indeed and not to be subject to demons anymore because
they are made to be subject to us.

9

FREE INDEED!

*If therefore, the Son shall make you
free, you shall be free indeed.*
JOHN 8:36

A COMMON AND MOST unfortunate outcome in deliverance is the situation whereby countless people who have experienced genuine deliverance fall right back under the dominion of the same demons from which they were delivered. To most people, this situation has been a great source of doubt, fear or discouragement, frustration, confusion, and sometimes hopelessness. The devil exploits these resultant attitudes to entrench two major lies, namely:

- Demons are invincible.
- The deliverance ministry is a futile exercise.

And unfortunately, by believing these lies a lot of people have found themselves in a cul-de-sac of unbelief and hopelessness. The underlying reason for such a deception is the demonically inspired ignorance about the nature of freedom in Christ and the fate of demons subsequent to a successful experience of deliverance. I do believe there is a great need for a clear understanding about the nature of freedom in Christ and the fate of demons following their expulsion from a human life.

There are at least two incidents in the ministry of the Lord Jesus Christ as documented in the New Testament that deal with the nature of such freedom and the fate of demons after deliverance. First, we turn again to Matthew 12:43, where Jesus says, "When the unclean spirit is gone out of a man, he walketh through dry places, seeking rest and findeth none. Then he saith, I will return into my house from whence I came out; and when he is come, he findeth it empty, swept and garnished. Then goeth he and taketh with himself seven other spirits more wicked than himself, and they enter in and dwell there; and the last state of that man is worse than the first. Even so shall it be also unto this wicked generation" (1).

In this cardinal statement, many vital facts are obvious.

First, demons do leave their victims when confronted with the name of the Lord Jesus Christ, under the power of the Holy Spirit.

Second, when they go out of their victim's body they go into dry places and wonder in search of rest. It is important to note that when demons leave their victim(s) they don't die because they are spirits and their ultimate destruction with Satan and other satanic forces is still in the future (Matt. 8:29; Rev. 20:10).

Third, because their desire for rest cannot be satisfied as long as they wander in the desert or wilderness, they invariably decide to come back to their "house." They are at least intelligent enough to make such a realization about the barren nature of dry places and the need to re-occupy the body of their past victim(s) in the absence of any other resting place. Only the bodies of living beings offer demons real shelter and rest.

Fourth, when they get back to their ex victim, their tactical priority is to explore the current spiritual state or condition of that person. The immediate post-deliverance state is described as empty, swept, and garnished. An alternative rendering is "unoccupied, swept and put in order" (Matt. 12:44). And having ascertained this state, they are desperate to get back in, dwell there, and find rest by recruiting additional demons more wicked than themselves. This reveals the degree of determination and desperation which demons exercise to entrench Satan's presence and purposes in a human life.

Fifth, thus the last state of the victim becomes worse than the first.

Sixth, this experience is typical of the overall satanic activity in the present generation and age.

The other incident that reveals the nature of freedom after deliverance is described in John 5:14. This was part of the encounter between the Lord Jesus Christ and the man He healed at the pool of Bethesda. Afterwards, when Jesus met him in the temple, He told the man, "Behold, you have become well, do not sin anymore, so that nothing worse may befall you" (John 5:14).

I personally see this as a parallel to what in modern medical practice is referred to as take-home or discharge instruction, which is a sound medical step often, employed to ensure a relapse-free recovery. Likewise, the prescription of Jesus in this situation is simple, precise, wise, and up-to-date divine counsel. In this prescription, my attention is particularly attracted to three realities:

"You have become well."

Healing and deliverance in the name of Jesus Christ are not just possibilities but present day realities. They are as attainable today as they were in the days of Jesus's earthly ministry—"Jesus the same yesterday and today and forever" (Heb. 13:8).

"...sin no more!"

Also, victory over sin is as real and up-to-date as healing and deliverance. This is God's expectation of everyone who has received healing and deliverance. Furthermore, this reality demonstrates the fullness of freedom in Christ.

"...a worse thing..."

Both healing and deliverance can be lost. Moreover, the resultant relapse may usually be worse than the initial condition. Any negligence or denial of the fact that both healing and deliverance may be lost mostly stem from ignorance about the nature of freedom in Christ.

In both of the cases reviewed above, the core lesson is that initial personal experience of healing, deliverance, and victory over sin are attainable in Christ, but a sustained experience of these is conditional. Moreover, real freedom goes beyond the initial experience of deliverance. Real freedom does not only entail a "symptom-free" life but the exercise of a sustained victory over evil and a new level of experience of worship and service to God. In the case of the man at the pool in Bethesda, his healing brought about significant triumphant reversals. He had a thirty-eight-year history of infirmity, which confined him to the pool at the sheep gate, resulting in physical dependence and emotional problems. He could not attend the temple feasts for those past thirty-eight years. However, after his encounter with Jesus, he arose, took up his pallet by himself, and walked. I see the climax of his freedom as his ability to walk himself to the temple and become part of the divinely ordained feast. The feast was part of God's heritage for him as a Jew; however, Satan kept him bound and out of the feast for thirty-eight years. In the counsel of Jesus, if he would continue to enjoy his newfound freedom, he would have to depart from evil and walk in the light from then on.

Likewise, for those in our age who have come to Christ Jesus and have received the grace of healing, deliverance, victory over addictions, besetting sinful habits, and all other forms of sin, God's purpose is not merely a change of our immediate condition or a cessation of the particular symptoms, manifestations, or experience of the bondage that we were under, but a new divine ability to walk in boldness and power, serving God without fear all the days of our life. It is in this way that we come to the fullness of His provisions, plans, and purposes in all things that pertain to life and godliness. It is as we progressively move away from corruption into the fullness of salvation that we appropriate God's divine nature and the glory that is in His Son Jesus (Heb. 2:9–10; 2 Pet. 1:1–10).

The deliverance we have in Christ should motivate us to an attitude and lifestyle of service and worship of the true God without fear and hindrance. Any motivation short of this is an abuse of grace, which robs God of His glory and opens us up to demonic attacks.

There is plenty of biblical counsel available to anyone who has received the ministration of deliverance. These spiritual measures will not only help build formidable spiritual defenses, but will also jumpstart some necessary aggressive and offensive spiritual exercise on a regular basis. This is the transition from bondage to dominion.

SUGGESTED STEPS TO CONTINUED DELIVERANCE

The following are suggested steps on how to keep your deliverance and come to real freedom from demons. Like the steps to deliverance, these suggestions are not routine legalistic, magical formula or doctrines, but biblically based tips.

1. Stay in Christ

The recipient of the grace of deliverance must put on Christ and remain in Christ if he or she is to experience continuing and full freedom. When a believer abides in Christ, the believer is hid in God; and the name of the Lord becomes a personal strong tower. This is the most secure position in the entire universe; a place and position so guarded with the divine fence of protection that no evil force dares penetrate. Moreover, when we as believers walk and live in Jesus Christ, we receive His righteousness, power and authority. These and other aspects of Christ's blessings and grace, when invested in the believer through fellowship, make the believer a terror to demons and other satanic forces.

To put on Christ means to believe in and proclaim Jesus as God's Son and Messiah who died on the cross for mankind and rose from the dead. This is a life of total identification with Him and public confession of Him. Such a confession and identification goes beyond verbal confession and implies a confessing with your whole lifestyle. It not only calls for witnessing but it also involves being a witness. When such a lifestyle is manifested in our daily contacts with our fellow humans—believers and non-believers—without compromise, God is glorified in Christ through us.

God's glory is the purpose for which we were created. Glory in this way reverses the Fall and its results. Wherever God's glory is made manifest, Satan and his forces lose their claims. Compromise weakens the believer's spiritual defenses.

> We know that no one who is born of God sins, but
> He who was born of God keeps him and the evil one
> does not touch him.
>
> —1 John 5:18

If we will continue to walk in the newness of life we have in Christ, He will empower us to walk in victory and keep us from satanic influences and attacks.

2. Be Spirit-baptized

Being baptized with the Holy Spirit is a valid spiritual experience and heritage in Christ Jesus that is fulfilled on two levels.

First, it is a definite and real initial experience following forgiveness of sins and the new birth. This was the experience of the early church on the day of Pentecost (Acts 2:1–13) and of the Gentiles of Cornelius' household when they received the gospel of grace (Acts 10:44–46). God expects all believers to have a definite experience of this divine person known as the Holy Spirit (Mark 16:17–18; Acts 2:38–39; 19:1–7). This initial impartation of the Holy Spirit upon the believer is what is commonly referred to as the Baptism of (with) the Holy Spirit.

Second, it is an expected moment-by-moment fellowship experience between the indwelling Holy Spirit and the believer. The priority God attaches to this experience underscores its unique value for success in every area and phase of Christian life. The New Testament records clearly show that the early church did regularly experience these fresh infillings or re-fillings (Acts 4:31). In Ephesians 5:18, Paul the Apostle enjoined believers as a matter of priority, "And do not get drunk with wine, for that is dissipation, but be filled with the Spirit."

At the believer's initial infilling, God puts a seal of ownership on the believer (1 Col. 6:18–19; Eph. 1:13–14). And to the extent that the believer appropriates that divine seal and ownership, to that extent also is Satan's hold over him or her broken. This Holy Spirit infilling is particularly needed for the victory, growth, and overall well-being of the recipient of deliverance. By this act of infilling, God's Holy Spirit comes to indwell and empower the believer. The Holy Spirit is a person, and not only does He have the desire to indwell the believer, but He also desires to have the believer yield all of his or her life and body to Him as a temple. Some of the specific works of the Holy Spirit in the life of the believer include:

- guidance into divine sonship (Rom. 8:14, 16)
- divine empowerment for prayer, worship, evangelism and testimony (Mark 16:17–18; Luke 4:45–49; Acts 1:8; 4:31; Rom. 8:26)
- revelation of divine truths and inheritance (John 14:16–18, 26; 16:13–15; 1 Cor. 2:9–16)
- healing of sickness and afflictions (Rom. 8:11)
- divine protection (1 John 5:18)
- power over demons (Mark 16:17–20)
- impartation of supernatural gifts and ability for spiritual exploits (Zech. 4:6; 1 Cor. 12:1–31)

All these and more are necessary for every child of God. Their importance and value to the one who was once tormented, manipulated, and dominated by demons in the past, and has now been delivered and desires to live in victory, is invaluable. Without such an ongoing personal relationship with the Holy Spirit, there cannot be any real and lasting freedom from demons. Such a continuing personal relationship with the Holy Spirit imparts His presence and power in a measure that destroys every satanic yoke (Isa. 10: 26).

3. Reckon your flesh dead

"Now those who belong to Christ Jesus have crucified the flesh with its passion and desires" (Gal. 5:24). The flesh, in this context, refers to the rebellious human nature, which was inherited from Adam after the Fall. It is also variously referred to in the New Testament as the old man (old self), the body of sin, and the body of the sin of flesh. This Adamic or sinful nature is the source of all sinful passions and desires in every human being. It is this nature in us that primarily makes us commit sins or sinful acts. By its very nature, our flesh is corrupt. The various expressions of its corruption are listed in Galatians 5:16–23, called the works of the flesh. The flesh is absolutely incapable of pleasing God because it cannot obey God's law. The best response the flesh can give to the law is sinful passions and desires leading to death (Rom. 7:5–7).

Furthermore, the sinful passions and desires of the flesh constitute a very conducive breeding ground for demons. The sinful nature and demons are not synonymous; however, the sinful nature is "demon friendly" and demons feed on its passions and desires.

God's plan for believers as far as the flesh is concerned is victory over its passions and desires. This is the unavoidable challenge to all Christians, especially those who have received deliverance from demons. The extent to which a believer can experience such spiritual victory depends largely on the extent of the believer's victory over the flesh. The basis for this crucial victory, and the ultimate solution to the problem of the flesh, is also revealed in God's Word. The revelation is that on the cross, the Lord Jesus Christ put the flesh to death and by His resurrection did bring forth in us the New Creation, or New Man. Whereas the flesh is the product of Satan's lie in us, the New Creation is on the other hand the product of the Holy Spirit, the nature of Jesus Christ, and His righteousness (Eph. 4:21–24, 25–31; Col. 3:10–17).

This new creation is God's new life in the recipient of deliverance. This is Christ in the believer who through death, resurrection, and ascension prevailed over the flesh—the old self.

There are three practical steps to exercising victory over the flesh on a regular basis.

First, recognize that the Lord Jesus Christ put the flesh to death on our behalf on the cross. In other words, our sinful nature was dealt with on the cross. All its demands and claims over us were met through the punishment Jesus bore on our behalf. Subsequently, in effect the flesh as a power or force has with all its claims been rendered ineffective. This fact is historical and real, and it has been so for over two thousand years. And as far as God is concerned, this was a done deal—"It is finished!" (John. 19:30; Rom. 6:6).

Second, reckon with the above stated historical fact truth. If you will regularly reckon with the fact of the death of the flesh on the cross, then you will realize in your personal experience today what had already taken place over two thousand years ago. This is the point of personal application of a general truth. No truth of the Word of God ever becomes effective in our individual lives until we personally reckon with the truth for our personal needs. It is not enough to know the truth, but the truth is only made effective when we personally identify with or reckon with and apply that truth. In other words, having known the truth, we proceed to personally ponder over it and in the process conclude the truth to be so for our need and in us at the present time. Once again, we need to reckon our flesh dead (Rom. 6:11, 13–16; 8:2; Gal. 2:20; 5:16–24; Col. 3:1–5). Only then will we be able to shun the appeal of the desires and passions of the flesh.

Third, we must then act on the known and reckoned truth. The logical result of received and reckoned truth is action. Action in this context refers to deeds appropriate or resultant to our faith. "Faith without works is dead" (James 2:20). In acting out our faith like Abraham, it becomes perfected by our works (James 2:21). And as far as our present theme of crucifying the flesh is concerned, the prescribed action is simple. Paul pointedly states it as follows:

Therefore, do not let sin reign in your mortal body that you should obey its lusts. And do not go on presenting the members of your body to sin as instruments of unrighteousness, but present your body to God as those alive from the dead and your members as instruments of righteousness to God (Rom. 6:12–13; Col. 3:5; Rom. 6:16–19).

These steps demonstrate the way God's grace operates to deliver us from the law, the flesh, and the power of sin. In other words, when we receive the revelation of the truth or fact of our deliverance from the flesh, and proceed to acknowledge or reckon with it, then we must act on the knowledge of that fact and the result is this, "Sin shall not be master over you, for you are not under the law but under grace" (Rom. 6:14).

You need to regularly take a stand and deny or say no to ungodliness, which includes all inner sinful attitudes, thoughts and outward sinful acts. Such a position sets you, the believer, apart from the dominion of sin, demonic manipulation, and bondage, and positions you in God's will. When we continue to reckon with the death of the flesh on the cross, we will keep the flesh dead and mortified. Our failure to reckon with the work of the cross and the death of the flesh keeps the desires and passions of the flesh alive and active. And demons thrive on such grounds.

4. Study and live by the Word

In God's arsenal, His Word holds a unique and tremendous importance. In fact, the Word of God is the foremost weapon of offense against all agents of Satan's kingdom. Following an initial experience of deliverance, Satan and his disgraced demons usually make frantic efforts to regain entry into and control over the life of their past victims. They bombard the minds of these persons and seek to assail them with all sorts of evil devices and weapons such as doubt, fear, guilt, condemnation, anxiety, depression, physical symptoms, and crisis in relationships, among other forms of harassment. In such situations, the foremost way the believer will triumph is by holding out the sword of the spirit, which is the Word of God. When scripture is spoken by faith against Satan and his forces, through testimony, praise, and prayer, God's ordained strength is released to silence the enemy and his forces.

Jesus's encounter with Satan in the temptation is a classical case., Satan thrice tried to tempt Jesus into disobeying the Father—and each time Jesus countered and neutralized Satan's arguments by standing upon and declaring the Word of God to Satan. Eventually Satan was defeated and had to leave the presence of Jesus (Matt. 4:1–10; Luke 4:1–13).

In Revelation 12:11, it was revealed that in the midst of the future cataclysmic encounter between God's forces and Satan's forces that the believers on earth overcame Satan with the blood of the Lamb and the word of their testimony. The word of their testimony, I believe, involves a proclamation of the Word's teachings concerning the blood. The implication, therefore, is for the redeemed to study, know, meditate, and live in obedience to God's Word so as to ensure its divine efficacy when spoken in faith against demons and other forces of the enemy in times of need (Josh. 1:8; Ps. 119:9–11, 46, 48, 67, 74; Matt. 4:4, 7, 11).

5. *Put on the whole armor of God*

One of the stark realities of the Christian life is the existence of wicked spiritual forces arrayed against the believer. (Some of these evil forces are enumerated in Ephesians 6:12.) In the light of this reality, Paul also impresses the reality of the believer's calling as a soldier of Christ (1 Tim. 1:18; 1 Tim. 2:34), who is involved in an ongoing spiritual insurgency. This is true of all Christians and of particular importance to the one who has been delivered from demons. The apostolic charge here is to be strong in the Lord. This entails a total commitment in Christ that avails us of His mighty divine power through His victory on the cross. This awesome divine power can be exercised with unspeakable results when the believer takes up the appropriate spiritual military dress code. Without this dress code, the believer will not only be ineffective in his or her spiritual offensives but also will be highly vulnerable to Satan's counterattacks.

Moreover, it must be emphasized that the armor does not drop onto the believer, but the believer takes up all the pieces of the armor by a decision of the will with the grace of the Holy Spirit. Some of the pieces of this armor as listed in Ephesians 6:14–18 include:

- Truth: honest and sincere living, without hypocrisy (2 Cor. 5:6–8; Eph. 5:11–13)

- Personal righteousness: manifested through a life of faith and love (Eph. 6:23; 1 Thess. 5:8)

- Gospel of peace: readiness and willingness to share the good news of peace made available by God to mankind through the life, death and resurrection of Jesus Christ (This is the proclamation of the simple, plain gospel to others who do not know Jesus Christ.)

- Shield of faith: exercising faith in God and His Word in every area of your life on a continuous basis to neutralize fiery darts, setting you and all around you apart from Satan's missiles

- Helmet of salvation: the deliberate exercise of hope in Christ amidst the prevailing tension and turmoil around you, involving an attitude of expectation of good, knowing that God is always in control even in the storm. It is a refusal to accept Satan's destiny for you, his gloom, depression, pessimism, doubt, foreboding of death and evil, and a refusal to yield to negative confessions and insinuations on a regular basis (Ps. 27:3; Jer. 29:11; 1 Thess. 5:8).

- Sword of the Spirit: involving the faithful study, meditation, obedience and proclamation of the Word of God: a constant attitude of faith whereby God's Word read, studied, meditated, and believed is thrust against satanic forces arrayed against you and against your spiritual and material inheritance. This is primarily an offensive weapon (Matt. 4:4–11; Rev 12:11).

- Prayer: the capstone. It is in and through prayer
  that all other weapons are activated, energized
  and released. Prayer, when combined with vigi-
  lance and fasting, binds Satan and his forces
  and demolishes all of Satan's evil plans against
  us. When you learn to pray regularly, you build
  a wall of protection around yourself and your
  family and also make successful aggressive
  incursions into Satan's territory. The effectual
  fervent prayer of the saint in the words of
  apostle James indeed avails much. The value of
  our prayer can be summed up thus: God the
  Father and Jesus the High Priest wait for our
  prayers to act on our behalf and on the behalf
  of others (Heb. 3:4; 4:4–16). God's angels are
  released and empowered by our prayers. Our
  prayers also restrain and hinder satanic forces
  and influences (Dan. 10). It is for the sake of the
  high premium that God places on our prayer
  that He appointed Jesus to be our High Priest
  and intercessor in heaven, and the Holy Spirit
  is sent to us to quicken and lead us to pray here
  and now on earth (Rom. 8:26–27). Our prayers
  not only leave Satan and his forces in shock
  and awe, but bind them with fetters of iron (Ps.
  149:8–9).

6. Get on the offensive

Following an experience of deliverance, the one delivered
is called into personal and corporate exercise of faith through
praise, testimony, evangelism, fasting, intercession, and all
manner of prayers. It is through these opportunities that he or
she reigns and rules with the enthroned King; Priest: the Lord

Jesus Christ. When we step into these ministries by faith, God our Father releases the rod of Jesus' authority into every situation where Satan and evil are at work. These are aggressive and offensive maneuvers appointed by God for us to nullify Satan's plans and purposes against us. Satan and his forces are not ignorant about this fact; they work tirelessly to manipulate us out of these divinely appointed opportunities. It is my prayer that God opens your eyes to this truth.

7. Burn the bridge

One of the most crucial moves in keeping your precious deliverance is to deliberately severe all links with your evil past. These pasts include occult practices, involvement in non-Christian religions, and cults and sects (even in Christendom) who reject the deity of Jesus Christ, the Godhead or trinity, the finished work of the cross, and other basic revealed tenets of biblical Christianity. Also, all links to your past wrong and immoral relationships, compulsive appetites, drives or addictions, and other sinful habits must be severed (Eph. 5:11–13). All objects and articles that remind you of or covenant you with your evil past, such as occult jewelry and literature, fetish objects, garments, charms, and symbols, must be burnt with fire. Bonfires remain the most effective way of cutting such links (Deut. 7:24–26; Acts 19:18–19; 2 Cor. 6:14–18; 7:1). You must also denounce past observances of all religious practices based on legalism, carnality, occultism, idolatry, new age, and philosophy (1 Cor. 2:1–2; Gal. 3:1–2; 4:3; 8–9; Col. 2:7–11, 13–19, 20–23).

Your reluctance or refusal to sever past evil links gives demons legal grounds to continue to harass you and also rob you of the Lord's protection. It is only in the position of obedience and faith that the blood of Jesus protects us. Outside of the light of this truth we are not guaranteed the protection of the blood (Exod. 12:21–22; 1 John 1:7; 1 Pet. 1:2).

8. Be water-baptized

One of the basic commands of the Lord Jesus Christ to the apostles in the Great Commission is that new believers must be baptized into Him by immersion in water (Matt. 28:18–20; Acts 2:38, 41). And in obedience to this ordinance, converts to Christ submitted to water baptism. Through this divinely ordained act of immersion, otherwise known as water baptism, every believer gets to experience a definite, initial public identification with Jesus Christ in His death, burial, and resurrection unto a newness of life, just in the same way Jesus identified Himself with our nature, sin, and judgment (Rom. 6:3–5; Gal. 3:27; Col. 2:12; 3:1). When we are identified with the Lord in immersion typifying the death of the sinful nature, we also symbolize in experiential testimony a newness of life—a resurrection life. This is subsequently and fully appropriated in our daily experience when we regularly reckon with this event (Rom. 6:11).

Moreover, like the baptism in the Holy Spirit, immersion in water has a unique value in the ministry of deliverance. To the recipient of deliverance, water baptism in many ways represents some form of separation from enemy satanic forces in the same way the Israelites were separated from the enemy Egyptian forces by their immersion and passage through the Red Sea (Exod. 14:20–31; 1 Cor. 10:1–6). Peter also typifies the experience of Noah and his household whereby they were transported in the ark through the waters from a world under demonic influence and judgment unto a place of safety in Christ Jesus. The lesson of this typology is that through water baptism, the believer is separated from a world controlled by satanic influences and under divine judgment, and carried over to a new life in Christ. Paul succinctly describes this experience as "a deliverance from the domain of darkness and a transfer to the kingdom of His beloved Son" (Col. 1:13).

I personally suggest that baptism by sprinkling during infancy is not recommended by the New Testament. The New Testament pattern was immersion of adults who have made a decision to follow Jesus Christ. I also recommend that anyone who has received salvation or deliverance should ask for immersion baptism even if he or she was sprinkled as an infant. On a more practical note, not a few people have experienced violent demonic manifestations while they were being immersed. In fact, in many evangelical charismatic circles, baptismal services do regularly and spontaneously involve the deliverance ministry. This is hardly an accident, since demons never feel at ease whenever they are brought face to face with the necessity and imminence of their separation from their victim through the power of the cross.

9. Testify

I believe that one of the major hindrances to the full manifestation of God's power in some lives and circles is the dearth of public declaration of the personal experience of God's salvation, healing, and deliverance. Many people have robbed themselves of God's power and blessing because of their failure to testify to God's power in their lives. Some who have received initial blessings of salvation have opened up greater surges of these blessings when they testified. On the other hand, many have lost their healing or deliverance due to their failure to testify.

The story of the lepers who received healing under the ministry of Jesus is a great lesson (Luke 17:11–19). Whereas the ten were healed, nine failed to testify. The only one among them who testified with thanksgiving was said to be "made whole." Testifying is a confession of God's goodness, power, and holiness. It glorifies God and silences Satan and his forces, who may seek to raise a counter attack on account of your testimony—but they will sooner or later be overcome.

Symptoms of sickness and demonic bondage do bow to our testimony of God's goodness and power. The devil, knowing fully the power of testimony, seeks to hinder a believer from testifying. He uses the devices of doubt, fear, discouragement, embarrassment, shame and pride. If you will sacrifice your pride and self-esteem and boldly testify to God's transforming power in your life, the blessings that await you are incredibly tremendous.

The people who came under the saving, healing and deliverance power of the Lord Jesus Christ in the Bible were not ashamed to testify. They were quick and bold to declare what the Lord delivered them from. Often times, they testified against the will of the religious authorities—so why shouldn't you? In fact, the beneficiaries of the ministry of Jesus did riot only verbalize their blessings on a one-time basis; they also regularly and openly identified themselves with the message and overall ministry of Jesus. The example set by a group of women in the ministry of Jesus is just one of the many impressive cases.

And it came about soon afterwards, that He began going about from one city and village to another, proclaiming and preaching the kingdom of God; and the twelve were with Him, and also some women who had been healed of evil spirits and sicknesses: Mary called Magdalene from whom seven demons had gone out, and Joanna the wife of Chuza, and any others who were contributing to their support out of their private means (Luke 8:1–3).

These women were not ashamed or embarrassed to have

their personal spiritual details disclosed in the Bible for the rest of time and eternity. In equal measure, the Lord blessed them tremendously. To Mary Magdalene the Lord first appeared after His resurrection. These women and many other people who came under the Lord's ministry became free indeed. This freedom is threefold:

- First, they were freed from demons, infirmities and other forms of Satan's power.
- Second, in addition, they became free to serve their new Lord Jesus by following Him and testifying of His power, goodness, and mercy.
- Third, out of this new life of freedom and discipleship came a new life of commitment, especially financial commitment by their giving to Him and His ministry out of their personal substance.

This threefold freedom is what the full gospel ministry is intended to achieve. If these women had not come under the deliverance and healing ministry of Jesus, they would have remained invalids under the yoke of demons and sickness, and would never have fulfilled their calling in the ministry of Jesus and in their personal and family lives.

Personal testimony also silences enemy forces and brings faith and deliverance to a completion. In the Epistle to the Romans, Paul says, "With the heart man believes resulting in righteousness and with the mouth he confesses resulting in salvation" (Rom. 10:11).

Salvation in this context also includes deliverance, but that comes not just by believing in the heart but also by confessing with the mouth. In this way with a firm assurance in the heart, the mouth finds liberty to testify even in the face of opposition, impossibility and skepticism, and God takes the responsibility of making it good. Our continuing testimony with thanksgiving, praise, and godly living always honors God, and to the one who glorifies God in this way, God will unfailingly show His complete deliverance.

> Whoso offereth praise glorifieth me and to him that ordereth His conversation aright will I spew the salvation of God.
>
> —Psalm 50:23

Earlier on in this study, we came to an understanding of the fact that though demons do leave when confronted by a genuine ministry of deliverance, they will muster every audacity at their disposal and methodically, persistently seek to regain what they call their house, the body of their ex-victim (Matt. 12:44). This counterattack is usually more ferocious than the original condition mostly because they reinforce themselves with seven more demons. This is most severe within the first two to three weeks of the initial ministration. Some of the more common devices that demons use at this stage are the persistence of some previous symptoms and feelings that necessitated the ministration of deliverance. Furthermore, Satan will bombard the mind of the individual with doubts about God's Word and concerning the effectiveness of the deliverance ministration received.

In some cases they cause the individual to be oversensitive to the point of searching for some new symptoms and feelings that may not exist. This may lead to confusion, fear, and panic. In such cases, the recipient of the blessing of deliverance must realize the following key aspects. First, this is a plain, simple intimidation strategy designed to overwhelm the spiritual defenses around their ex victim's mind. Second, all that the delivered one needs to do is to be settled in mind that his or her deliverance was effective since it was based on Christ's finished work on the cross.

The effectiveness of ministration should not necessarily be measured by persistent or new symptoms, feelings, or subsequent attacks. The delivered person must put on a mindset of victory by reckoning or bearing in mind that the offending demons left when they were commanded to leave. By the exercise of your mind and spirit in this way with the right confessions expressed through testimony, thanksgiving, praise, authoritative prayer, and worship, you will call off the demons' bluff and they will flee.

In the language of Paul the Apostle, this is being strong in the Lord and in the strength or power of His might. This is why we as Christians put on the full armor of God, "Standing firm against the schemes of the devil" to "withstand the wiles of the devil" (Eph. 6:13). This is how to submit yourself under the mighty hand of the Lord and resist the devil in order to see him flee (1 Pet. 5:7–9). If you fail to exercise faith in this way then demons will, through your fears and doubts, chase you out of your blood-purchased victory. Always bear in mind that on the basis of the finished work of the cross and in your position as a child of God redeemed by the blood of Christ, demons are subject to you.

I must emphasize one more time that deliverance and freedom are not always synonymous. Deliverance is a tool and process of bringing about a condition or state of freedom. Deliverance gets the demons evicted, and freedom takes advantage of the new condition of the human spirit, which is empty, swept, and kept in order and appropriates the divine provision of regeneration, the indwelling and the outpoured Spirit, and the abundant opportunities that exist in true Christian fellowship and relationship. In the state of freedom, the believer having experienced a release from demons and related symptoms proceeds to serve God in holiness and without fear (Luke 1:74–75; Acts 7:7).

10

A MINISTRY OF THE HOLY SPIRIT

T HE DIVINE MANDATE to cast out demons is primarily the operation of the Holy Spirit. This is so both in the personal earthly ministry of the Lord and that of His church (Luke 4:14–19; 24:49; Acts 10:38). In contemporary language, this ministry of the Holy Spirit is often described among evangelicals as the "deliverance ministry," and the one who regularly operates in this grace is often referred as a "deliverance minister." Within liturgical and non-Christian circles, the word *exorcism* is used to describe this practice, while the one who operates in exorcism is referred to as an exorcist.

The practice of exorcism in most cases suggests a free world where even unbelievers and other charlatans operate with all sorts of unscriptural or extra-biblical methods. Many who have no personal commitment and relationship with the Lord Jesus Christ attempt to cast out demons. The most typical example is the case of the seven sons of Sceva as revealed in the Books of Acts, But also some of the Jewish exorcists, who went from place to place, attempted to name over those who had the evil spirits the name of the Lord Jesus, saying, "I adjure you by Jesus whom Paul preaches. 'Seven sons of one Sceva, a Jewish chief priest, were doing this'" (Acts 19:13–14).

Clearly, there was a culture of exorcism, which the sons of Sceva represent. That they had no part in the Lord or His ministry and divine authority was a fact known to these demons; hence they refused to listen to them. Moreover, this exorcism movement was contemporaneous with the genuine ministry of deliverance in Paul's gospel ministry in Ephesus.

The fact that this form of exorcism seeks to parallel the genuine operation of the Holy Spirit in the casting out of demons was also evident when the Pharisees accused the Lord Jesus of casting out demons by the power of Beelzebub. The Lord confronted them with the fact that while He himself cast out demons by the anointing of the Holy Spirit, their sons indeed were the ones who practiced exorcism by Beelzebub (Matt. 12:24–28).

This indicates that when demons are cast out, either the Holy Spirit or Beelzebub is at work. For the Lord and the church, the anointing to cast out demons is of the Holy Spirit (Matt. 12:28). The power behind exorcism as practiced by anyone who has no personal faith and relationship with the Lord Jesus and who employs non-biblical methods is Beelzebub. Every genuine deliverance ministry will do all of the following:

- Accept and exult Jesus Christ as the Son of God and Lord
- Accept His finished work on the cross as the only basis of redemption and righteousness with God
- Depend on the Holy Spirit as the only source of genuine supernatural power for ministry
- Rely on God's Word as the only source of revelation and doctrine
- Receive the ministry of deliverance as a ministry gift from God and not to be commercialized.

Any ministry that denies these and the other basic biblical tenets about the Lord is of Beelzebub and should not be patronized by the church.

Exorcism by Beelzebub is not only ineffective but it is also known to lead those who patronize it into covenant with demons. It does in some cases offer very marginal and temporary relief outwardly, but inwardly there is always a deeper initiation of the one seeking help into the dark world of Satan's kingdom. This is the typical modus of practitioners of non-biblical exorcism as revealed by Isaiah the prophet, "For thou hast abandoned thy people, the house of Jacob, because they are filled with influences from the east and they are soothsayers like the Philistines and they strike bargains with the children of foreigners" (Isa. 2:6).

Those who seek to operate in the ministry of deliverance or dabble in exorcism without any personal relationship with the Lord are typically soothsayers, and the pervasive contemporary eastern or new age influences have greatly thrust them to prominence. They lead people away from the Spirit of the Lord and into darkness.

THE MINISTRY OF DELIVERANCE

Since this operation of grace was not described in the Bible in words like *deliverance ministry* and *deliverance minister,* many have for this reason developed a skeptical attitude towards it. In some cases their argument was based on the fact that neither the lists of the gifts of the Holy Spirit in 1 Corinthians 12 and 14, nor the list of New Testament ministries in Ephesians 4 and 1 Corinthians 14 made mention of any ministry or gift of deliverance or office of a deliverance minister; yet in the entire course of the church's history, the Holy Spirit has consistently used believers to cast out demons. The question, therefore, is how we solve this terminology puzzle.

A Gift of the Holy Spirit

After a considerable time of prayerful consideration, I have personally come to an understanding and conclusion that the operation of the Holy Spirit to cast out demons through the believer is a combined operation of some of the gifts of the Holy Spirit discussed in 1 Corinthians 12. These nine gifts are referred to as the manifestations of the Spirit. In other words, these are the various aspects of the nature, power, and activities of the Holy Spirit expressed through the believer (1 Cor. 12:7). The nine specific manifestations are:

1. a word of wisdom
2. a word of knowledge
3. the gift of faith
4. gifts of healings
5. workings of miracles
6. prophecy
7. discerning of spirits
8. diverse kinds of tongues
9. interpretation of tongues

These gifts are divinely imparted upon believers whom the Holy Spirit has set in the church to accomplish His various purposes (1 Cor. 12:8–11, 18).

The gifts of the Holy Spirit are not only for those in ministry offices but also offered to all believers who will open themselves to receive in faith (1 Cor. 12:2–31; Eph. 4:11; Heb. 2:2–3). Yet this question is often asked: which of the nine gifts of the Holy Spirit is the casting of out demons a part of?

Based on the revelation of God's Word and personal experience, I believe the operation of the Holy Spirit to cast out demons is primarily a combined operation of three gifts of the Holy Spirit: the gift of discerning of spirits, the gift of faith and the gift of workings of miracles.

1. Discerning of Spirits: This gift represents the foremost manifestation of the Holy Spirit wherever and whenever demons are at work. Through this gift the believer is able to recognize the presence and activity of demons, identify specific demons by name and function and also to differentiate one demon from another. It is also of tremendous value in determining the progress of ministration and to determine when the demons have been expelled. The value of this gift is underscored in its operation in the deliverance ministry of the Lord, the apostles and the present generation of believers. For instance, when demons spoke through a man in a Capernaum synagogue, the Lord was able to discern the presence and activity of demons in the Man and also effectively differentiated between these evil spirits and the man's spirit, hence He was able to say "Be quiet and come out of him" (Mark 1:23–26).

It was also with the aid of this vital gift of the Holy Spirit that the apostle Paul was able to see beyond the impeccable confessions about his person and ministry by the slave girl in the city of Philippi and identify a demon of divination. (Acts 16:16–18) It was only after he had in this way identified the spirit of divination in the girl that he exercised the gift of faith to cast the demon out resulting in the miracle of deliverance. In this case, as in the case of the Lord's ministry in the synagogue in Capernaum, the apostle Paul said to the spirit "I command you in the name of Jesus Christ to come out of her!"

(Acts 16:18). So the pattern is that the Holy Spirit through this gift in the believer, identifies and exposes a demon, isolates it from the personality of its victim and confronts it through the gift of faith, and workings of miracles. And in the course of ministration other gifts are released as the need arises. The operation of this gift is not limited to the ministry of deliverance. It also operates to identify the person, presence and activity of the Holy Spirit, angels and the human spirit.

2. Gift of Faith: This is not the faith that results in initial salvation. It is neither the "measure of faith" given to every believer for a moment and daily victory in Christian living, nor the fruit of faith (faithfulness) of Christian character. The gift of faith is a special kind of faith, a supernatural faith made available to the believer with which to move mountains. It is an operation of God's own faith by the Holy Spirit through the believer to deal with impossibilities (Matt. 21:18–22; 17:14–21; Mark 11:12–14; 20–25). This gift like the others is not limited in its use to the ministry of deliverance. However, it is indispensable in this ministry where it is usually expressed as a prayer of authority or a word of command (Mark 1:21–28; 11:14; Acts 16:16–18). When used in ministering healing, it is referred to as a prayer of faith (James 5:14–18). Whenever commands are issued with divine faith in the heart and in the name of the Lord Jesus Christ against demons, they get rebuked, bound, and evicted. They must bow and leave (Phil. 2:9–11). When the gift of faith is in operation, the gift of the workings of miracles is often if not: always simultaneously activated as demons begin to manifest and leave, healings result, and other supernatural signs are precipitated. So in ministering deliverance, the main trigger is the gift of faith followed immediately by the workings of miracles.

3. Workings of Miracles: This is the third primary gift of

which the casting out of demons is part. It is an operation of the Holy Spirit through the believer whereby God's power is made manifest in a very dramatic way to counter and neutralize Satan's presence, power and work. This gift is referred to in literal Greek as "works of power." It is often triggered by and works together with the gift of faith; they are almost always inseparable. The word *miracle* as used here is *dunamis* in Greek. In its noun form it is *dunastes*, meaning "one who exercises dominion or authority."[1] In this case, the believer thus endowed exercises the Lord's kingdom authority and dominion over Satan and his agents, such as demons. Such authority or dominion manifests the defeat and helplessness of demons and destroys their works.

'Whenever this gift is exercised in the New Testament, the activities of demons are usually exposed and reversed. As a result of this, there exists a pattern in the New Testament whereby the exercise of this gift is often associated with the operation of the ministry of deliverance from evil spirits. When it does not operate, in cases where demons are at work, deliverance from demons seems not to occur. For instance, in the ministry of the Lord Himself in His own hometown, the following experience was described, "And He could do no miracle there except that He laid His hand upon a few sick people and healed them" (Mark 6:5).

In this case, there was clearly no case of demons being cast out; only a few sick people were healed by the laying on of hands. The Bible clearly says there was no miracle. Some may ask, but isn't healing a miracle? The answer is that generally speaking healing is a miracle, but strictly speaking not all divine healings are considered miracles. Some of the differences between miracles and healings are as follows:

- Miracles are of a broader nature and deal with much more than the healing of sicknesses.

- Miracles (including miraculous healings) are more dramatic or instantaneous and obvious to the senses; whereas many forms of divine healing are gradual in nature and often involve inner body organs that are not immediately visible to the senses. Furthermore, in many cases miracle healings involve a re-creation of a diseased, damaged or removed body part.

There are several other instances in the Bible in the Lord's ministry and that of the early church of some healings that required demons to be cast out. (Such are cases of healings by workings of miracles recorded in Matthew 4:23–25; 8:16; 10:1, 8; Mark 1:32–34; 3:10–11; 6:12–13; and Luke 4:40–41; 6:17–19; 7:20–22; 8:1–2; 9:1–2.) While in other cases of healings, only hands were laid and a prayer of faith offered for the people for healing. The casting out of demons was not applied (Matthew 5:13; 8:1–4; 9:1–8; 18–26; 20:29–34; Luke: 17:1–19; John 5:1–15; 9:1–12).

We should also not lose sight of the fact that the working of miracles is not only about diseases and healing. The spirit of God also uses it to intervene in other areas of need. This, I believe, is the main reason why workings of miracles and healings are listed as different gifts of the Spirit.

Another case in the New Testament where the gift of workings of miracles directly dealt with demons is in the ministry of Philip in Samaria: 'And the multitudes with one accord were giving attention to what was said by Philip, and the signs (miracles) which he was performing" (Acts 8:16). Through the workings of miracles the Holy Spirit directly confronted, exposed and neutralized the power and work of those demons.

Hence the next verse says, "For in the case of many who had unclean spirits, they were coming out of them, shouting with a loud voice, and many who had been paralyzed and lame were healed" (Acts 8:7).

Please notice the direct connection between the gift of workings of miracles in verse 16 and the expulsion of demons from their victims in verse 17. Furthermore, when the demons were expelled, some form of miraculous (or dramatic) healings simultaneously took place. In verse 13 of Acts 8, an occult practitioner and a strong man over the city was brought face to face with the power of the Holy Spirit through the operation of this gift in Philip, and was freed from demonic bondage. He lost his occult power when demons of occultism left him and he believed in the Lord.

In the ministry of Paul in Ephesus, the gift of the workings of miracles was also mightily in operation and the result was that demons were cast out in droves and dramatic miracles of healings were rampant. However, it must be noted that gifts of faith and of workings of miracles never operated in isolation.

SECONDARY GIFTS

For the casting out of demons to be much more effective, there are other invaluable though not primary gifts. These include a word of knowledge, which may provide supernatural information about the condition; a word of wisdom for a supernatural strategy; and a gift of healing to deal with specific sicknesses. The gifts of diverse kinds of tongues, interpretation and prophecy can be used to rebuke the enemy and also announce victory, comfort, and edification. What a gracious advocate and divine helper we have in the sovereign Holy Spirit. Casting out of demons is, indeed, a ministry of the Holy Spirit.

A Word for the Minister

The ministry of deliverance usually demands commitment, discipline, patience, and consecration. It is not in the interest of anyone called to this ministry to meddle with unprofitable works of darkness.

> And do not participate in the unfruitful deeds of darkness but instead even expose them; for it is disgraceful even to speak of the things which are done by them in secret.
>
> —Ephesians 5:11–12

It is important that you, the believer, live under grace, so when demons put up a challenge saying, "I recognize Jesus, and I know about Paul, but who are you?" (Acts 19:15), you are able to silence them. Despite all their bluffing, demons recognize the authority of the Lord over them and also are acquainted with much torture, shame and defeat at the hand of the Lord's servants. Believers need to abide in Christ and follow the teachings of the apostles. Remember that the seven sons of Sceva had none of these; hence the demons attacked and overcame them.

These expectations, when met, not only make this ministry effective but also position the ministering believer to better appropriate his or her much needed divine protection, fellowship, refreshing, and more anointing. I would personally suggest the following points for the consideration of those involved in the ministry of deliverance:

1. Separation from any known sin or work of the flesh, and from compromise with evil

2. Regular self-examination so as to identify and eliminate attitudes of resentment, bitterness,

inordinate ambition, pride, self-righteousness,
legalism carnality, lust, fear guilt, unforgiveness,
competition, jealousy, self-centeredness, judging,
exaggeration, dishonesty, and exploitation

3. Lifestyle characterized by prayer, fellowship, fasting,
and systematic Bible study

4. Prayerful sensitivity at all times, in every situation, exercising a level of discernment that is able
to clearly distinguish between good and evil, as
well as constant prayer to claim protection over
God's interests and God's people, including self
and family. Also remember to pray before and
at the end of every session, for the leading of the
Holy Spirit and protection for self, relations and
all involved in the session including the person(s)
being prayed for.

5. Openness to teamwork for purposes of effectiveness of ministry and mentoring others or being
mentored by others, including accountability and
responsibility to other ministries and Christians,
which are invaluable safeguards

6. Basing teachings and methods on scripture: When
undue emphasis is placed on personal or cultural
experience and other subjective issues, objective
Bible truth gets blurred and many come under
confusion and frustration. Obsession with super-
stitious attitudes becomes rampant. These may
indeed launch some into greater bondage instead of
deliverance.

Final Recommendations

Acknowledge the presence and power of the Holy Spirit to deliver. Depend on Him and be sensitive to His leading from start to finish of a deliverance session. The exercise of the gifts of the Holy Spirit is vital to effective ministry; a word of wisdom, word of knowledge, discerning of spirits, workings of miracles, healing, faith, and diverse kinds of tongues are of tremendous advantage. The anointing of the Holy Spirit acknowledged, received, and exercised in this way breaks every yoke.

A persistent declaration of the power of the cross, the blood and the name of the Lord Jesus Christ as revealed by the Word are of immense expulsive power against demons and of more demolishing impact to the power of darkness than any nuclear weapon in the physical world. For small group ministries, especially when ministering one-on-one to some one of the opposite sex, the assistance of an extra hand is recommended. I further recommend that where possible, someone of the same sex with the recipient of deliverance be present.

When deliverance is ministered by a team, it is necessary to have a defined leadership system; this will, among other things, reduce the tendency of conflicting commands to demons by the various members of the team. Orders issued to demons must be clear, precise, and unambiguous. Avoid long conversation or interviews with demons. When conversation becomes necessary, it should be short and purposeful, such as demanding the name, nature, and source of the demons involved.

Never accept fear, intimidation, mockery, slander, resistance, or revelation of or threat of mishap or evil destiny from the demons. In such cases rebuke and silence the demons and cancel every evil plan thus revealed. Ask for the Lord's protection upon everybody in the arena and its vicinity, and cut off every channel of demonic re-enforcement by a prayer of authority. Avoid distractions and a hasty attitude; ministering deliverance requires patience.

An atmosphere of thanksgiving, praise, and worship of the Lord Jesus Christ releases a tremendous level of anointing during ministration. Gentleness, decency, and an attitude of confidentiality are extremely important.

Why Could We Not Cast It Out?

As discussed before, some cases of demonic bondage recur after deliverance had been administered. Some such situations can be blamed on the victims' inability to keep his or her deliverance due to failure to follow guidelines suggested in the previous chapter. However, there are cases whereby the demons clearly resist eviction. These are intrinsically difficult cases but not hopeless and insurmountable. A typical example is presented in the case of the lunatic epileptic in Matthew 17:14–21 and Mark 9:14–29. In the account in Mark 9:18, the father of the boy said this about the disciples: "I told your disciples to cast it out and they could not do it." Matthew 17:16 renders the account thusly, "They could not cure him."

After reproving the disciples for their doubt and unbelief, the Lord personally cast the demon out of the boy. When the disciples enquired from the Lord, "Why could we not cast it out?" the Lord blamed their doubt and unbelief, and also recommended fasting with prayer in these words: "This kind does not go out except by prayer and fasting" (Matt. 17:21). In the Lord's wisdom, therefore, while there are difficult cases, such stubborn demons behind them must succumb to faith expressed with fasting prayer. Apparently, fasting greatly intensifies faith and boosts authority and the gifts of the Holy Spirit. Throughout scripture, fasting has proved to be a consistent spiritual means of dealing with difficult situations in the life of a believer.

Fasting is a basic kingdom responsibility required of every believer by the Lord (Matt. 6:16). Those in the early church who were involved in the gospel ministry, which includes deliverance and healing, fasted often (2 Cor. 11:27). Furthermore, those in the ministry of deliverance and healing today need to give themselves to fasting and prayer, knowing that some demons will not go except by fasting. This does not in anyway suggest that every case of deliverance demands fasting.

11

CAN A CHRISTIAN HAVE DEMONS?

W HEN MOST CHRISTIANS are brought face-to-face with the reality of demons, one commonly posed question is whether a Christian can indeed be demon possessed. This question usually springs from a wide range of religious attitudes, such as opposition to the doctrine of demonology and the ministry of deliverance. In some cases, there is a form of resentment towards preachers who teach and minister deliverance on a regular basis.

There are also cases of sincere, open-minded believers who just get "turned off" from the truth of deliverance because of the extreme and unbalanced emphasis on the theme of deliverance and demonology by some overzealous believers or preachers. Also, there have been cases of abuse, exploitation, and manip-ulation associated with the ministry of deliverance. However, we need to bear in mind that almost all other genuine Chris-tian doctrines or experiences have their own share of abuses. Generally, the reluctance among many believers in accepting this truth can also be blamed on the misunderstanding of some basic doctrines of Christianity such as sin, salvation, the flesh or Adamic nature, and the spirit world.

Another source of difficulty and confusion is the use of inac-curate or inappropriate terminologies in dealing with certain subjects on the theme of deliverance and demonology. I will at this point, on the basis of biblical facts and experience and by the grace of God, attempt to offer some clarity and understanding. In answering the question of whether a Christian can be demon possessed, it would be helpful to examine the key concepts of possession of the human body by spirits, deliverance, and healing in relation to the salvation experience, the contemporary salvation message, and confusing terminology.

POSSESSION OF THE HUMAN BODY BY SPIRITS

In considering this question, the concept of spirit possession of the human body is central, especially when we are dealing with the nature of spirits. It is very crucial to note that both the Holy Spirit and demons indwell, possess, and influence their hosts. Once the question of ownership is established, the spirit involved goes on to exercise indwelling, possession and influence. This is how the operating spirit initiates and maintains control.

In bringing this further down to personal experience, we need to remember that God, the Father of Jesus Christ, created every man and woman on earth; but not every person on earth has yielded to God and made Him Father and Lord. Scripture also makes it clear that those who have not received Jesus as Lord and Savior have rejected the Fatherhood of the true God over them and are therefore under the fatherhood of the evil one (Matt. 13:38; John 8:38–45; Acts 13:10).

Unbelievers may still appear normal, outwardly clean, and may or may not be bound by a habit or addiction. They may or may not be overtly troubled by demons and they may in fact be religious; but in the words of John the Apostle, as long as such a person refuses to yield to Jesus the Christ, he or she has no right to call Jehovah Father (John 1:11–13). Equally, the Spirit of God does not claim possession over him or her. The Holy Spirit only lays claim to those who have made Jesus their Lord.

The unsaved person is under Satan's fatherhood and can be said to be demon possessed. However, the good news is that such a person does not have to remain in these states. He or she may become a child of God through personal faith in the Lord Jesus Christ (John 3:1–12; Rom. 8:28; Eph. 2:2; Heb. 2:10–11).

Conversely, a born-again Christian is a child of God. He or she is not possessed by Satan or demons, but by the Holy Spirit. The Holy Spirit possesses the believer the moment he or she receives Christ Jesus by faith (John 1:11–13). The Holy Spirit is God's seal or token of possession upon the believer (Eph. 1:13–14; 4:30). So as God's children, born-again Christians are possessed and sealed by the Holy Spirit.

By this provision and as long as the believer remains yielded and committed to Jesus as Savior and Lord, no one else besides almighty God can lay claim to him or her; not even the believer can lay claim to his or her own life. In this light, the apostle writes, "Ye are not your own" (1 Cor. 6:19, KJV). The Holy Spirit in the born-again believer is not just an external trademark or seal, but as sovereign Lord He transforms the body and life of the believer into a temple and indwells there.

Doctrinally speaking, the possession of the believer by the Holy Spirit is very real, but the full realization of this truth experientially depends on the believer's moment-to-moment, daily fellowship with the Holy Spirit, which leads to the progressive yielding of the believer's life and body to Him. This is worked out through a life of obedience. The result of such consecration will lead to continual separation from evil and dedication unto God. A life so filled with the Spirit of God will experience the outflow of praise, thanksgiving, worship, prayer, witnessing, and exploits. In such a life, the fruit and gifts of the Holy Spirit will feature not only without measure, but also effortlessly. In other words, beyond the initial confession of faith in the Lord

Jesus Christ and the baptism in the Holy Spirit, there is a need for a moment-to-moment consciousness of the Holy Spirit's presence with and in the believer in every place, manifesting a lifestyle of obedience, love, and faith.

> For all who are being led by the Spirit of God, these are the sons of God.
>
> —Romans 8:14

Our initial confession of faith in Christ makes us God's children babies, as it were. But God desires to have mature sons and daughters. This is one of the purposes for which the Holy Spirit was given: to bring us to maturity. Spiritual maturity is the stage of spiritual development when we can perceive grace and appropriate God's perfect will and provision for us (Gal. 4:1–3).

Suffice it to say that the believer's failure or refusal to yield to the leading of the Holy Spirit not only robs the believer of his or her inheritance in Jesus Christ, but also opens him or her up to Satan's claims, demonic invasion and attacks. Nothing should replace or substitute the ministry of the Holy Spirit in the life of the believer. Any form of religion or religious activity that denies or rejects this ministry brings about carnality and legalism, dependence on the flesh and law in place of the Holy Spirit. Ultimately, both carnality and legalism are promoted by evil spirits and incur God's wrath upon those involved.

Bear in mind that legalism and carnality are not limited to non-Christian religious groups but do show up from time to time in the lives of some Christian believers and whole congregations. A more frightening sequel to legalism and carnality is apostasy, the renunciation of Christian belief. In Jeremiah 17:5 the Lord says, "Cursed is the man who trusts in man and makes flesh his strength, whose heart departs from the Lord."

In other words, there is a curse from God upon anyone who turns from the Spirit of God and trusts in the flesh (carnality), especially through the instrumentality of the law (legalism). Historically in Israel under the law and thereafter, in the life of the church, whenever someone turns from the Holy Spirit as God's appointed revelator and helper, they turn to the law or to the human nature. This is usually to their detriment. Unfortunately, at such a point of crisis and weakness, demons or evil spirits can penetrate an area of the believer's life or inheritance. This is one way a Christian can have a demon or come under demonic influence. This dilemma existed among early Christians and Christian groups, and it exists today.

We will now proceed to consider some incidents in the New Testament whereby some Holy Spirit-baptized individuals or groups were at risk of coming under demonic influences and in some cases did come under such influences.

1. Ananias and Sapphira

In Acts 4, it was revealed that this couple was involved in some form of deception. There was no doubt they were both born-again, Spirit-filled believers. They were a part of the earliest Spirit-filled Christian community whose conduct and faith were described in Acts 4:32–37. However, shortly afterward Ananias lied to the Holy Spirit. And just before the judgment of God fell on him, Peter, the apostle under the power of the Holy Spirit, summed up the situation as follows: "But Peter said, Ananias, why hath Satan filled thine heart to lie to the Holy Spirit?" (Acts 5:3). The apostle clearly indicates that Ananias yielded his thought life to Satan and as a result came under the influence of demons; hence he could come up with such lies. Lying is not of the Holy Spirit but of demons. Thus if a believer fails to yield to the Spirit of God, he or she opens a way for demons to "fill" at least some area of his or her life and in this way exercise their influence in and through that believer. It is possible to argue that Ananias was not demon possessed but that he was apparently influenced by demons or demonized. He yielded his heart to demons and they influenced his actions.

2. The Galatian Syndrome

The Christian believers at Galatia could be considered one of the finest groups of Christians in the early church until the incident that warranted Paul's epistle to them. The progression of their full gospel experience may be summed up as follows.

First, they came to Christ and were in Christ through the hearing with faith the true gospel Paul had preached (Gal. 2:6–9). Second, they were Spirit-baptized or Spirit-filled and were obedient to the Holy Spirit through the gospel. Moreover, they regularly witnessed miracles and other powerful manifestations of the Holy Spirit through their faith in Jesus Christ. Third, and tragically, having begun in the Holy Spirit, they did not remain in the Holy Spirit but turned to the flesh (carnality). Fourth, carnality (a "foolish attitude" of trusting in the flesh) opened them up to the demonic influence of witchcraft and demons of witchcraft and they got "bewitched" and further drifted from the reality and power of the cross (Gal. 3:1). Having drifted so far from the cross, they turned themselves over to bondage under weak and beggarly elemental spirits especially through legalism (trusting in law) and other forms of religious attitudes. Concerning this situation Paul laments, "Howbeit then, when ye knew not God, ye did service unto them, which by nature are no gods? But now, after that ye have known God or are known of God, how turn ye again to the weak and beggarly elements (spirits) whereunto ye desire again to be in bondage" (Gal. 4:8–10).

It is clearly stated that these believers came to the Lord Jesus Christ from an idolatrous Gentile background, and that they received the Holy Spirit with full divine supernatural witness; yet afterward they progressively began to ignore the presence of the Holy Spirit and the power of the cross. Instead of continuing in the divine provisions of God, they turned to the flesh and the law, both of which opened them up to the spirits of witchcraft and other forms of elemental spirits. As soon as these Holy Spirit-filled believers yielded to witchcraft and elemental spirits, their destiny changed from liberty to bondage.

One may also ask, "How can Christians ever come under bondage?" or "How can witchcraft ever operate within a Spirit filled congregation?" But the sad truth is that this tragic experience repeated itself many times in church history and still repeats itself among Christians today. The unvarying principle is this: when Christians reject the Holy Spirit and His provision they open themselves up to various kinds of demons. To the extent that they reject the Holy Spirit and His provisions, they also yield to demons and their evil influences. This is how a Christian can have a demon or come under demonic influences and bondage. But the good news is that repentance and forgiveness with restoration are all possible.

3. Paul's warning on apostasy

In his letter to Timothy, Paul shares a powerful, up-to-date prophetic vision with a focus on some spiritual activities in the church. He writes, "Now the spirit speaketh expressly, that in the latter times some shall depart from the faith, giving heed to seducing spirits and doctrines of devils" (1 Tim. 4:1–3, KJV).

In this prophecy, it was actually the Holy Spirit speaking to His people through Paul. Essentially, the concern is that some born-again Spirit-filled believers will depart from the Christian faith; they will no longer believe in the crucified and resurrected Christ as revealed by the Holy Spirit. This is similar to the Galatian situation; and as they turn away from the Holy

Spirit, they will automatically be opened up to seducing spirits (demons). Moreover, these people may still be in the professing church, saying the right things and singing the right Christian songs. Some may even minister in the five fold ministries and operate in the gifts of the Holy Spirit. In the last day, however, Christ will say, "Depart from me, I never knew you" (Matt. 7:21–23).

4. Discerning of spirits

God in His wisdom expects us to cultivate discernment. Moreover, He bestows upon us a particular gift known as discerning of spirits. This gift is listed along with the other gifts of the Holy Spirit in 1 Corinthians 12:1–11. Undoubtedly, this gift was meant for the use and benefit of God's people in the New Testament—the church. The gift of discerning of spirits basically is an operation of the Holy Spirit through a believer whereby the believer identifies or recognizes the spirits at work in a given situation or place. Also by the exercise of this gift, the believer can differentiate the presence and work of God's Spirit from that of other spirits. There is ample evidence in scripture to suggest that this grace was applied in ministry both within and outside the church. If there were no possibility of demons infiltrating the personal lives, families, and congregations of some believers, why would God bother to endow His church with such supernatural gifts?

In Paul's second epistle to the Corinthian believers, he clearly warns that a Christian believer may receive "another spirit."

> We receive another spirit which ye have not received.
>
> 1 Corinthians 11:3–4

When Paul talks of another spirit, he is referring to a spirit different or contrary to the Holy Spirit. He is clearly referring to a demon of religious deception. The question you may ask at this point is, "Can one receive another spirit after being Holy Ghost filled?" Once again, the answer is a clear yes! If a believer yields himself or herself to a spirit other than the Holy Spirit, he or she stands to receive such a spirit. The writer of the epistle to the Hebrews also indicates that the exercise of discernment trains the believers' spiritual senses to discern good, the work of the Holy Spirit, and evil, the work of evil spirits.

From the foregoing incidents, we may summarize that unless the necessary spiritual precautions are taken, a believer who is filled with the Holy Spirit may through careless ways yet open an area of his or her life to the activity of evil spirits. There are many practical experiences in the lives of believers that illustrate this. For instance, if a believer turns to a lifestyle of lying, addiction, or other negative habits, he or she will soon be or already may have been under the power of demons responsible for those acts.

It ought not to be, but like the apostle James pointed out, a Spirit filled believer who has one tongue may use that tongue to bless God and at some other times uses it to curse men, thus blaspheming the same God (James 3:8–11).

DELIVERANCE AND HEALING IN RELATION TO THE SALVATION EXPERIENCE

I believe like most other Christians that, when Jesus died and rose from the dead, He dealt a final defeat to Satan as well as to his principalities and demons. Jesus also by that singular act forgave the sins of humanity, healed their diseases, revoked curses, and made available to mankind all God's blessings.

The healing that Jesus worked out for us on the cross is perfect and complete, just like His forgiveness of our sins.

The deliverance He wrought on the cross was also perfect and complete. We must bear in mind that Jesus made every divine blessing available to us by one sacrifice, at one time, for all ages in time and eternity.

> By one offering (sacrifice) He has perfected forever them that are sanctified.
>
> —Hebrews 10:14

If Christ healed all on the cross two thousand years ago, why do many Christian believers fall sick today? Definitely, it is not because this sacrifice of Jesus mediated by the Holy Spirit has been weakened by historical circumstances and the passage of time—never! It cannot be weakened because it is a perfect sacrifice sealed by the eternal Spirit (Heb. 9:14). There are, therefore, other reasons why believers do fall sick today, but I will just suggest one.

I believe that the commonest reason is disobedience to God's Word through sinful acts and habits, as well as violation of God's standards for rest, sleep, exercise, diet, and purity. In the experience of King David, such a straying from God's Word is not salutary, "Before I was afflicted, I went astray but now I have kept your word" (Ps. 119:67, 1). He goes on to add, "It is good for me that I have been afflicted, that I might learn thy statutes" (Ps. 119:71, 1). And even more clearly, he states, "Fools because of their transgression and because of their iniquities are afflicted. Their souls abhorreth all manner of meat and they draw near unto the gates of death. Then they cried unto the Lord in their trouble and He saved them out of their distress. He sent His word and healed them and delivered them from their destructions" (Ps. 107:17–20).

Moreover, experience has shown that most of the infirmities or afflictions that believers are oppressed with today are demonic in origin, although this doesn't necessarily imply that all who are afflicted with such infirmities are living in sin. Still, through the ministry of deliverance most of these believers who have endured these infirmities for long have received healing and deliverance. If a believer can fall into sin or fall sick, it is also possible that such a believer can be demonized if he or she yields to demonic influences. Disobedience can bring sin, sickness, and demonic activity back into the life redeemed by the Lord. It is in this sense that a Christian can come under the influence of demons.

THE CONTEMPORARY SALVATION MESSAGE

Over the years, the church at large has vacillated on the salvation message. The core salvation message—the message of the cross—has been modified many times over to suit the various manmade doctrinal interests of the various denominations or streams of Christendom.

In God's plan, the message that brings salvation is the "gospel" or "good news of the kingdom." It is a message that proclaims the person of Jesus Christ as God's only begotten Son. It also proclaims and demonstrates the power of the crucified and resurrected Christ over Satan, demons, and their works: namely sin, sickness, poverty, curses, and oppression. This is the core objective as revealed in the Gospels, the Acts of the Apostles and the Epistles. These constitute the various facets of the Great Commission.

In other words, as we observed earlier on, both Jesus and His disciples in their ministry confronted people with the full gospel. They preached repentance from sins, healed the sick, cast out demons, and led new converts to water baptism and Holy Spirit baptism.

Unfortunately, at various periods in our contemporary age

most preachers only present repentance from sin, and when people believe, they present water baptism only as an option. These new converts are often not prayed over for deliverance, healing, and Holy Spirit baptism. The eventual result in most congregations is a large number of believers plagued by sicknesses and demonic oppression, not living in the power and gifts of the Holy Spirit. If we study the ministries of the early disciples, we will easily notice that new converts were prayed over for healing and deliverance at first contact with the gospel. The ministries of Philip and Paul are just two examples (Acts 8:5–12; 16:16–18; 19:11–12; 18–20).

It is encouraging, however, to testify that this pattern is now being restored in many parts of the world. Until this pattern is significantly restored, we will continue to pray for believers for deliverance from demonic oppressions they have endured since the time they believed.

Let me close this section by giving a biblical picture. Paul ran into a group of believers, and on discerning that they had not been Spirit baptized, he asked them whether they had received the Holy Spirit. When they expressed their ignorance about Holy Spirit baptism he proceeded, without any theological arguments or prejudices from either side, to lead them into the initial experience of Holy Spirit baptism (Acts 19:1–7).

Ignorance, doctrinal prejudice and pride, when not readily dealt with in humility, can rob us of wonderful blessings. While we should henceforth seek to present in earnest the full salvation package—the message of repentance, healing, deliverance, and baptisms—we should not deny the fact that our past and ongoing haphazard presentation of the gospel has left in our midst many believers who are still plagued by demonic oppressions, spirits of infirmity, and other forms of demonically inspired struggles that they came with from the world to the

Lord. In this kind of situation, it is the responsibility of the church to exercise the divine mandate of casting out demons and laying hands on the sick, if the church must come to its glory in readiness for its bridegroom the Lord Jesus Christ. Once again, let us be mindful of the fact that when people come to Christ, they come with the demons, sicknesses, habits, and struggles they endured while in the world; and these demons don't automatically go away. If they are not dealt with sooner through the ministry of deliverance and healing there will always be in the church Christians who are under demonic influences or can be said to have demons.

TERMINOLOGY

As I briefly mentioned before, terminology is one more cause of difficulty for many people in trying to make sense out of the idea that a Christian can come under demonic influence. The basic argument by those who question this assertion is that a Christian who is supposedly possessed by the Holy Spirit cannot be possessed by demons. Many Bible scholars attribute this confusion to the use of the expression "demon possessed." This expression is mostly used in the King James Version and few other English versions of the Bible. Most people contend that to address someone as "demon-possessed" implies complete ownership by Satan. However, since Jesus owns every sincere believer, the phrase "demon-possessed" is not applicable in the case of a believer. Furthermore, it is observed that in the original New Testament Greek, the three phrases commonly used to describe the activity of demons in a life are these:

- To be demonized (Matt. 4:24, 8:16, 28, 33, 9:32; Mark 1:31, 5:15; Luke 8:36)

- To have an unclean spirit (Matt. 11:18, Mark 7:25, Luke 8:27)
- To be in an evil spirit (Mark 1:23, 5:2)

In conclusion, whereas Satan and his demons cannot claim possession over a believer, yet a believer can open a door for demons or yield some area of his or her body or life to demons and in this way come under demonic influence or torment with such results as emotional or physical illnesses, inward pressures, struggles, or bondage in certain areas of his or her life. In such situations the Christian, in addition to counseling, prayer, fasting, and other forms of personal ministry, needs to come under a valid ministry of deliverance.

In other words, any Christian who at any time senses a need to come under a valid ministry of deliverance as a means of receiving God's provision of freedom, healing, or prosperity should refuse to be deterred by any hindrance such as doubt, unbelief, fear, shame, terminology, stigma, or embarrassment. These are some of the devices Satan employs to keep his victims from their inheritance of freedom in Christ. The ministry of deliverance, in this case and if rightly applied, simply constitutes an opportunity for a prayer of agreement through which the one in need and the one ministering draw upon God's all sufficient grace for healing and freedom.

Epilogue

THE ESSENCE OF DELIVERANCE

I N ALL OF our pursuits, secular or spiritual, when the essence of an activity, exercise or blessing is not defined and kept in focus, there's bound to be failure, disappointment, frustration, and sometimes destruction of self or others. When the essence is kept in focus, vision results and "where there is no vision a people perish" (Prov. 9:8).

One major hindrance to godly vision and purpose in life is self-centeredness. God's purpose for humanity through the deliverance ministry is to set the captives free. Complete freedom leads to the yielding of the human spirit, soul, and body to the lordship of Jesus Christ, culminating in holiness, peace, and joy in the Holy Spirit. If, after receiving God's wonderful offer of deliverance, you turn back to self, sin, and bondage, then you expose yourself to worse things in life a greater bondage (John 5:14).

God's purpose at creation was that humans would increase, multiply, and subdue the earth, ruling over the other creatures. The first Adam lost this purpose; the last Adam, namely Jesus Christ, restored it. Yet Satan works ceaselessly to make us blind to this precious fact of restoration. Paul explains this spiritual blindness as follows, "And even if our gospel is veiled, it is veiled to those who are perishing, in whose case the god of this world has blinded the minds of the unbelieving, that they might not see the light of the gospel of the glory of Christ, who is the image of God" (1 Cor. 4:3–4).

This passage of scripture exposes Satan's strategy in holding humans in bondage. The ultimate plan of Satan is to keep us from knowing and obtaining our possession in Jesus Christ. Hence Satan promotes ignorance: "My people perish because of lack of knowledge" (Hosea 4:6).

When we are deprived of our possession in Christ, we perish. Our needs are only met in our God-given possession, and we will never be complete until we possess our possessions. In Obadiah 17, this process is summed up: "But upon Mount Zion shall be deliverance, and there shall be holiness and the house of Jacob shall possess their possessions."

As I understand it, when God's people (Zion) receive the fulfillment of the promise of deliverance, they are brought to a place of holiness. If they continually yield to the "spirit of holiness," they shall possess their possessions. In Galatians 5, we were warned of the conflict between the spirit and the flesh. If we yield to the flesh, we will be open to the invasion of demons, which also bind and defile. This counters God's purpose for us as stated in Obadiah 17. Jesus Himself taught us to "seek God's kingdom first and His righteousness and every other thing shall be added unto you" (Matt. 6:33).

When the deliverance ministry flushes out demons, the Holy Spirit moves in to establish God's kingdom. Thus God's righteousness is revealed in us, and if we continue to yield to the Holy Spirit, He will continue to administer all of God's estate to us.

Deliverance is not the ultimate end; it is rather a gateway to holy living in submission to the Holy Spirit, who administers all of God's provision in Christ to the believer. God's provisions are our inheritance. They will become our possessions when we receive by faith our deliverance and walk in God's estate of promises by continuing in obedience to the Holy Spirit. This is the divine purpose and goal of deliverance.

TESTIMONIES

I WANT TO TESTIFY to the delivering power of the Lord God Almighty in His Son, the Lord Jesus Christ in my life.

I was born and raised in the city of Benin, Nigeria. My religious background was idolatry with particular emphasis in ancestral worship and animism.

My personal experience of demonic oppression began at the age of eighteen. Late one evening, as my younger brother and I were walking along a wooded path in my village, I suddenly felt a strange touch on my right foot. Initially I thought it was just one of those random bodily feelings, but when I got home I began to experience all kinds of bizarre feelings in my entire body. I felt changes in my body that I cannot explain fully. I got extremely alarmed when I suddenly felt an electrical shock-like feeling all over my body.

I was rushed to the hospital where I was admitted for treatment. A thorough medical checkup was carried out on me, which yielded no relevant results. From that point onward, I was never the same. I was continually bombarded with ever-increasing varieties of bizarre and bodily emotional feelings and changes. I also noticed a very strange pattern to my symptoms—they were unexplainably most severe on Tuesdays.

I was taken to several occult practitioners and witch doctors for a solution, but with each visit my situation grew worse. At one point, an occult practitioner I was seeking help from insisted I had to be initiated into his cult before I could be set free from the bondage and oppression I was under. On the scheduled day of initiation, I had been made to partake in a blood covenant (using human blood), whereby a group of us shared our blood by drinking it. After that I was brought before an idol in a molten image and was led into reciting certain covenant words laced with curses binding me to the idol and cult membership. Not only did my symptoms worsen, but I also realized that with each contact with an occult practitioner, witch doctor, or cult in quest for help and deliverance, I was getting deeper under demonic bondage through occultism and idolatry.

I came to the point of hopelessness, fear, discouragement, confusion, and depression as family members began to give up on me. I even began to have suicidal thoughts. But glory to God for His timely intervention as a pastor from my mother's congregation came for my rescue. He took me to church, led me to the Lord Jesus Christ, and prayed the prayer of faith over me, casting the oppressing demons out of me in the name of Jesus Christ.

From that day my journey began as a redeemed soul and born-again Christian knowing freedom, peace, and joy in Christ.

However, after I relocated to the United States in February of 2001, I backslid and began to live a life not pleasing to God, engaging myself in immorality and by doing so I opened the door for those evil spirits to return and invade my life once again. This time I even experience worse symptoms than those I had experienced in the earlier episode. At that time, out of fear of reliving the torment and horror of my past experience of demonic bondage, I began to consider suicide, feeling there was little point in living.

But once again, the good Lord intervened and led me to Pastor Isidore Agoha of Triumphant Life Church (TLC). My first visit to TLC was a Thursday night deliverance service in November 2003. When Pastor Isidore made an altar call for healing and deliverance, I came out confused and sick. After I briefly explained my situation, he rededicated me to the Lord Jesus Christ and began to pray for my deliverance from demons. Suddenly I felt a repulsive power between the man of God and me, which threw me to the ground where I lay vomiting. I could hear him continue to command every demon to leave me in the name of the Lord Jesus Christ and the power of the Holy Spirit.

Since that day I have not only remained delivered and free, but I have since married and now am a father of two beautiful children, all by the Lord's grace.

I say to all who hear this story, remain in Christ—never turn your back on Him, because the consequences are not worth experiencing.

To the Lord God be all the glory.

—O. A.
PENNSYLVANIA, USA

———◆———

Today I give all thanks praise, adoration, honor, and glory to the Lord God Jehovah, the God of Abraham, Isaac, and Jacob. He delivered me from the dominion of Satan and the oppression of demons through His Son, the Lord Jesus Christ.

I was born and raised in a Roman Catholic family, but over these several years while I was a practicing catholic, and as others were seeking better careers, families, and other prospects, I was busy looking for sleep. I was constantly under some serious demonic attacks that I will not be able to describe fully in this piece. For the most part I was harassed by humans (males and females) and several creatures: dogs, cats, snakes, and goats in my sleep. I was always fighting in my sleep and several times I was almost choked to death. Initially, these night attacks occurred only two or three times a month, but in 2006 it became frequent and unbearable.

After such nightmares in the night, I would feel their impact in all over my body the next day. My skin would burn as if I was placed on a grill. I developed a severe case of acid reflux whose cause could not be ascertained medically. All prescribed medical tests that I underwent for my overall condition yielded no helpful clues.

Emotionally, I was constantly controlled by fear, uncertainty, hopelessness, doubt, unhappiness, tension, resentment, anger, and worthlessness. Life for me became unbearable. I could no longer sleep in my house for fear of these attacks and then it dawned on me that I needed urgent help. I became desperate in my quest for help.

During this period, my younger sister, a born-again Christian who resides in Nigeria encouraged me to join a Bible-teaching church. A pastor friend of mine who lives in the Bronx and who was constantly praying for me advised me to accept Christ as my personal Savior. Friends and relatives that were aware of my situation kept urging me to give my life to Christ, yet I remained evasive. I began to honor their invitation, but every time I attended a Pentecostal church service, the attacks became more serious and dangerous.

In March 2007, I attended a service at Triumphant Life Church, a deliverance and healing ministry located in the Bronx at the invitation of a couple who are friends of mine. As soon as I entered the building I experienced a different atmosphere. I became emotional, peaceful, and felt encouraged to stay for the service. I truly enjoyed the service and at the end of the service, the couple who invited me took me to greet the pastor. After a brief moment of greeting, Pastor Isidore Agoha asked if he could pray for me to which I responded yes. And as soon as he laid his hand on my forehead I passed out. When I awoke, I realized I had been slain in the Spirit. As I was helped back on my feet, I felt lighter and peaceful.

After I left the service, and later that Sunday night, while asleep in my home, I felt a big snake gradually wrapping itself around my body. Being awakened by this, I ran out of my bedroom and into my living room and quickly turned on all the lights in my house. I did not return to my bedroom for the next two days for fear of a repeat experience. The following Sunday, an inner voice threatened me with greater punishment if I returned to Triumphant Life Church, although the pastor had encouraged me to come back. In fear of further retaliatory attacks, I went back to the Catholic Church. However, at the insistence of my friends, I returned to Triumphant Life Church for a deliverance and healing service as part of their annual Passover/Resurrection celebration.

It was Saturday, April 7. 2007. While I was standing in the prayer line, and as Pastor Agoha was praying for others before me, I felt a very unusual power take over my body. It swept my feet off the floor and I passed out and fell on the floor. When his assistants brought me up, pastor Agoha got to me and prayed over me and I went down on the floor a second time and passed out in the Spirit realm where I personally witnessed a war between God and Satan break out over my life. I felt I was in a distant world and could only hear the pastor's voice from a great distance, commanding yokes be broken from me and demons to come out of me.

As I was lightening up from my "unconsciousness," I realized I was on the floor that whole time, on my back, kicking the air and the floor with all four of my extremities. I heard myself scream, "I am free! I am free! I am free!"

When I got up from the floor, Pastor Agoha asked me, "How do you feel now?" I responded, "I feel like a truck had just been lifted off my shoulder!" and then I busted into more shouts of "I am free!" with both arms held high in the air. I was told later the entire episode lasted about forty-five minutes.

On April 11, 2007, I experienced another attack, but this time I called on the name of the Lord Jesus Christ in my sleep, as Pastor Isidore had instructed me beforehand, and I was instantly victorious.

Ever since, I have continued to experience peace, love, and happiness I had never before known in my life. I regained my self-control, and was blessed with freedom from anger and hopelessness. I am now full of hope and faith, without fear or doubt.

Not only was I delivered from demons, but I now have dominion over them.

God has indeed redeemed me, cleansed and washed me with the blood of His Son Jesus Christ. He has also endowed me with His anointing, gifts, and placed me under the ministry of His servant, Pastor Isidore Agoha.

I am presently a minister in training at Triumphant Life Church.

To God be all the glory!

—S. E.

New York, USA

The moment I received a copy of Pastor Agoha's new book, *Demons Are Subject to Us*, and began reading it, I realized that it was published for me.

When I got to the section describing a claim by demons referring to the human body as a place where they reside, my body started jerking, my muscles contracting. I stood up and continued reading. When I got to the section on the occult and false religion, a sensation of heat appeared inside my body. My clothes became heavy on me, but I continued to read. At that point I knew there was a power tussle between two spirits inside of me.

When I began to confess my belief in the Godhead, the Trinity, and the divinity of Jesus Christ, I began to feel myself bending over. As I continued to bow, I began to itch and dropped to the floor. My actions overwhelmed me, but I refused to let go of the book and continued with concentration to confess my faith in the divinity of the Lord Jesus Christ, His virgin birth, His death on the cross, and His burial, resurrection, and ascension.

To God be the glory, I am delivered and healed today.

—Sister C.
Maryland, USA

Author's Note:

Sister C. was oppressed with infertility and repeated miscarriages before she obtained a copy of this book. However, after her deliverance, she was able to conceive and is now blessed with a baby by the power of the Holy Spirit, in the name of the Lord Jesus Christ.

NOTES

CHAPTER 4—DAIMON

1.   David M. Dosa, M.D., M.P.H., "A Day in the Life of Oscar the Cat," *New England Journal of Medicine* Volume 357:328-329, Number 4 (July 26, 2007), Web site: http://content.nejm.org/cgi/content/full/357/4/328, accessed July 20, 2009.

CHAPTER 5—BROKEN BORDERS: PART I

1.   Author's paraphrase from Web site: www.ourladyswarriors.org/dissent/defnewage.htm, accessed July 20, 2009.

CHAPTER 10—FREE INDEED!

1.   *Merriam-Webster's Collegiate Dictionary*, Eleventh Edition (Springfield, MA: 2003).

ABOUT THE AUTHOR

Isidore A. Agoha is the senior pastor of Triumphant Life Church and president of Calvary Campaign Ministries International (CCM), both based in the Bronx, New York City. Pastor Agoha and his wife, Maureen, received the apostolic vision to launch a ministry where believers are taught and imparted with keys to triumphant Christian living.

Pastor Agoha regularly reveals to members and visitors of Triumphant Life Church the fundamental truths of God's Word with practical exercises of kingdom living and authority. Calvary Campaign Ministries is the global outreach ministry of Triumphant Life Church based on Acts 26:18, "To open their eyes, and to turn them from darkness to light, and from the power of Satan unto God, that they may receive forgiveness of sins, and inheritance among them which are sanctified by faith that is in me."

Pastor Agoha holds a master's degree in Nurse Anesthesia from the University of New England. Pastor Agoha and his wife are blessed with three beautiful children.

TO CONTACT THE AUTHOR

The pastor is available for conferences, retreats, seminars, revivals, counseling, and other speaking engagements. Please contact him at:

Triumphant Life Church
3048 Holland Ave.
Bronx, NY 10467
(718) 231-1604

E-mail: contact@tlcny.org

Web site: www.tlcny.org

To order from Triumphant Life Church's catalog of CDs/DVDs and other literature/materials from Pastor Agoha's ministry, please call 877-234-0590.